IS LIFE WORTH LIVING?

IS LIFE WORTH LIVING?

Some Thoughts on the Message of Ecclesiastes

CHRISTOPHER BREARLEY

Published by Zaccmedia
www.zaccmedia.com
info@zaccmedia.com

Published October 2016

Copyright © 2016 Christopher Brearley

The right of Christopher Brearley to be identified as author of this work has been asserted
by him in accordance with the Copyright, Designs and Patents Act 1988.

ISBN: 978-1-911211-40-2

British Library Cataloguing-in-Publication Data
A catalogue record for this book is available from the British Library.

Zaccmedia aims to produce books that will help to extend and build up the Kingdom of
God. We do not necessarily agree with every view expressed by the authors, or with every
interpretation of Scripture expressed. We expect readers to make their own judgment in the
light of their understanding of God's Word and in an attitude of
Christian love and fellowship.

CONTENTS

Introduction

Is life worth living if nothing we pursue has any permanence? What does one have to show for it at the end? Will the dead live again? Regrettably, only a few people ever seriously consider these vital questions. Many are so busy that they do not have time to stop and think about anything important. It is sometimes said that we live in an age where machines are becoming more like people, and people are becoming more like machines; unable to think for themselves. Some people do not even want to think because they have no desire to confront the various problems associated with life and death. They bury their head in the sand – a saying that describes someone who ignores their shortcomings or those of others – and readily accept the proverb that 'ignorance is bliss'. But such a belief is questionable. Another proverb aptly reminds us that 'not to know is bad, not to wish to know is worse'.

This is good advice, for running away from a situation by evading facts is never a positive way forward. It is foolish to pretend that things are fine when they are not.

Is life meaningless? Or does it have a purpose? And if it does have a purpose, how is it possible to experience life in all its fullness? That is why I have written this book. I want you to join me on a great journey of discovery. It is a journey that has been travelled by numerous others, in every generation, with varying degrees of success or failure. That being so, is not the lesson to be learned very clear? It is to learn from the experience of those who have gone before. Surely, there is no good reason for us to repeat their experiments. What is the point of trying to reinvent the wheel? Any attempt to do so would be a complete waste of time, diverting our attention from accomplishing something much more worthwhile.

Clearly, time does not stand still; the circumstances of life are very different from one generation to the next, but basic human nature does not change. What can you point to that is new? It has all been done before. All too often, however, people ignore the important lessons of history and learn by their costly mistakes in the school of experience, whose colours are black and blue. Now, I know we all make mistakes and that is how we often learn about what not to do. Even so, there are many instances when it is best to learn from someone who has already been along the road we intend to take.

There is a book in the Bible that is written primarily to encourage us to use our eyes, as well as our ears, to carefully observe and question the purpose of life. This book is called Ecclesiastes. The authorship is traditionally accredited to King Solomon, writing towards the end of his life, reflecting on life's experiences and the lessons learned. Not all scholars, however, would agree with such a claim. They would argue that it was written long after Solomon's day. Who, then, was the author? The answer is that we are not told, nor is there a need for us to know. The human author is not particularly important, whilst the message which deals with everyday life, is. Ecclesiastes speaks a necessary message for today because, I believe, it can direct us to the true meaning and purpose of life.

It would probably be fair to say that a casual reader of Ecclesiastes could easily reach the conclusion that it is nothing more than a pessimist's diary of despair, or an abyss of disillusionment. This is because the author's personal reflections on life and the world repeatedly emphasise the monotonous meaninglessness, the vanity, of earthly things. These he considers to be short-lived and to offer very little while one has them. His wealth, his wisdom, his works and his world all appear to be meaningless. That is why the German poet, satirist and journalist Heinrich Heine (1797–1856) called Ecclesiastes the 'Song of Scepticism' (*Das Hohelied der Skepsis*). But for anyone to say that this book is a confession of total failure by an old man who has reflected deeply upon life is surely an unfair assessment. Rather, I would suggest that it is a stern warning against placing excessive confidence in the momentary things of this world. Earthly things swiftly pass away, and often offer very little while one has them.

Our life on earth is relatively short when compared to the overall picture. Probably most people reach a physical peak during their mid-twenties and from then on deteriorate both physically and mentally. The older we become, the faster the deterioration, until eventually we die. This is a depressing picture if extinction is the only certainty confronting us all. But is it? Do we have to live with something that has no reason at all, and which therefore leaves us bewildered?

The following pages contain a series of observations that will hopefully challenge us to carefully consider and evaluate the important issues of life. Therefore, are you ready for the journey of exploration that may lead to satisfaction? If so, fasten your seat belt and be prepared for a tough and uncomfortable ride over a tortuous route in a dangerous and hostile world. In spite of that, persevere, enjoy the search, and discover how the meaningless can become meaningful. Discover if you are getting the most out of each day, and living life to the fullest!

GOING NOWHERE

'Meaningless! Meaningless!' says the Teacher. 'Utterly meaningless!
Everything is meaningless.'
What do people gain from all their labours at which they toil under
the sun?
Generations come and generations go, but the earth remains for
ever.
The sun rises and the sun sets, and hurries back to where it rises.
The wind blows to the south and turns to the north; round and
round it goes, ever returning on its course.
All streams flow into the sea, yet the sea is never full.
To the place the streams come from, there they return again.
All things are wearisome, more than one can say.
The eye never has enough of seeing, nor the ear its fill of hearing.
What has been will be again, what has been done will be done
again; there is nothing new under the sun.
Is there anything of which one can say, 'Look! This is something
new'? It was here already, long ago; it was here before our time.

(Ecclesiastes 1:2–10)

THE EARTH CAN BE LIKENED to a stage that endures to the end of time. People appear upon it and then, after a relatively short period, pass away to be replaced by their successors. What they have been left by other people, or gained by their labours, will be left to others. It is clearly futile to try to hold on to anything under the sun for, in the end, it will all be taken from us. The time of our enjoyment of worldly possessions is very short. Everything in an earthbound life is transient. This leads us to ask the question: 'What is the purpose of it all if nothing we pursue has any permanence?' Surely, it is utterly meaningless, like chasing the wind.

What do people really gain from all the hard work they do here on earth? This is a reasonable question that has been frequently asked in every age and in every country. Do they achieve anything worthwhile? Is it not a fact that when people are born they do not bring anything into this world, and when they die they take nothing out of it? Materialistically, our entry and our exit are identical. Thus we could say that our pilgrimage on earth is nothing more than a journey between two periods of nakedness. How do we ultimately benefit from all our hard labour if at best we live for a few decades and then we are gone? Is life worth living?

Does your view of life as a whole ever appear to be rushing in circles and going absolutely nowhere? Do you ever feel that life's running you instead of you running it? The answer of many people would be a resounding: 'Yes!'

So it is not surprising that life is sometimes likened to a treadmill; it goes round in a continual cycle and the result is that you always finish where you began. The quicker you move, the quicker it goes, but however fast, it always ends in the same place. After running a long and tiresome race you are no nearer your goal than when you started. As a consequence, everything in life can appear, to the mind of a rational being, to be going in circles and getting nowhere. Is life meaningful or meaningless?

The natural world clearly exhibits repetitiveness. Phrases such as 'life cycle' or 'come full circle' plainly describe the cyclical view of life and nature. What goes around comes around again and again in generation after generation. The sun rises at dawn and the sun sets in the evening, and repeats this process day after day, but what does it actually accomplish? Its cycles end where they began. The wind can change its direction but it cannot blow in any direction which it has not often blown before. It continually moves from point to point, to no apparent purpose, ever returning on its course. Similarly, streams of water join with others in their onward flow, widening and deepening until they reach the sea, yet the sea is never full. Water constantly evaporates into the sky to form clouds which then produce rain. Thus the water returns to the place from which it came.

This continual circularity of nature continues year after year and so it can become very wearisome.

Our minds are as restless in their pursuits as the sun and the wind, but never satisfied. Like the sea, our senses are continually fed, but never filled. Whatever we see or hear, we are not content. There is always an insatiable desire for diversity and for something new. Adults often behave like children, always eager for a new toy because they soon grow weary with what they have. They dislike old things for no other reason than that they are old, and want new things for no other reason than that they are new. They are possessed by an appetite for novelty.

'New' is one of the most tempting words in our vocabulary; that is why it is so often used in the advertising world to grab our attention. Some people are continually searching for something new; assuming that if it is new it must be better. For instance, the package tour industry is continually trying to tempt us with new and exotic destinations. Adventure holidays or visits to faraway places are offered which claim to be new and exciting challenges. In a similar way, the fashion industry tries to tempt us with new designs. Fashions continually change. Clothes go out of fashion and then they return to be the latest craze.

The above are just two common examples of how people are constantly searching for something new so as to attain satisfaction. But there is nothing new under the sun. This is not to deny the inventiveness of humankind or that there are changes for better or worse. Rather it emphasises the monotonous circularity of human activity and the fact that history repeats itself. All the events which happen to people are basically the same as have happened to others before them. What has been will be again, what has been done will be done again. Material things by themselves have never ultimately satisfied or solved the fundamental problems of life, and never will. So I urgently want to know if it is possible for anyone to find true happiness and lasting satisfaction in a materialistic world.

Midlife crisis is a term coined in 1965 by the Canadian psychoanalyst and organisational psychologist Elliot Jaques.[1] It is a condition where people awaken to the fact that they have reached life's halfway stage and this focuses their minds upon the future. They may believe that they have accomplished very little, if anything, worthwhile, in either their job or personal life. It is a frank recognition of: 'What do people really get for all their hard work?' Everything appears to be utterly meaningless! This, and the deep awareness that it is probably too late to start again, can result in anxiety and even a prolonged period of severe depression. It may be triggered by a dramatic life change such as divorce, financial hardship, shattered dreams, bereavement or redundancy. Sometimes, however, there appears to be no apparent reason for this deep sense of hopelessness.

Certainly life can be extremely wearisome for those who are trapped in a constant routine of doing things. Getting up and going to work in the morning, returning home in the evening and then later going to bed may be likened to a treadmill. Many people feel that they are going nowhere and achieving nothing. This constant battle to achieve a desired target in life, and a concern that it is unlikely to ever be achieved, can result in despondency and dissatisfaction. It is also equally true to say that great success does not necessarily satisfy. Many people have reached a pinnacle of so-called success, only to be stranded there.

When we look in a mirror at ourselves and reflect upon what we have achieved, what do we see? Do we see a reflection of a person who is concerned, maybe even frightened, about the future? One of the biggest fears many people face is the fear of death. Is life worth living if everyone must die and that is the end of it all? Or, when we look in the mirror, do we see a reflection of success? And we might ask, 'How do we define and measure success?' As we shall see in the next chapter, there are four primary routes in life that people try to achieve this success with varying degrees of satisfaction. Are you now ready, after a brief pause, for stage two of our journey of discovery?

A pause for thought

The writer of Ecclesiastes does not attempt to evade the many difficulties and perplexities of life. To what extent would the same be true of you? Are you satisfied and content, or concerned about the future? Why is this?

THE SEARCH FOR SATISFACTION

I denied myself nothing my eyes desired; I refused my heart no pleasure.
My heart took delight in all my labour, and this was the reward for all my toil.
Yet when I surveyed all that my hands had done and what I had toiled to achieve,
everything was meaningless, a chasing after the wind; nothing was gained under the sun.

(Ecclesiastes 2:10,11)

W E LIVE IN A WORLD WHERE many people are dissatisfied. Despondency, disillusionment, dissatisfaction, depression and despair are a common feature of life, because the selfish and shallow joys of materialism and the acquisitive society are usually considered to be the only way to happiness. Nothing could be further from the truth. History repeatedly reveals that contentment is not derived from material possessions, but from activities where personal advancement is not the primary motive.

Within life there are four major routes that are frequently tried to attain lasting satisfaction. These are: education, employment, enjoyment and enrichment. The author of the book of Ecclesiastes diligently tried all of these without success, as do some people today. What can you point to that is new here on earth? It has all been done before. History merely repeats itself, so what, therefore, are we to do?

Studying history is worthwhile for all of us because the past provides lessons for the present and guidance for the future. The English statesman, orator and writer Edmund Burke was right when he said: 'In history, a great volume is unrolled for our instruction, drawing the materials of future wisdom from the past errors and infirmities of mankind.'[1] History enables us to learn from the experience of others; their successes as well as their failures. Regrettably, the German philosopher Georg Wilhelm Hegel also got it right by saying, 'Peoples and governments never have learned anything from history, or acted on principles deduced from it.'[2] People today tend do the same things, reach the same conclusions, and make the same mistakes as those who have gone before them.

The four major roads toward satisfaction

Education

The major aim in life for many – especially young people – is to achieve an academic goal. Their lives can become dominated by the desire to accumulate knowledge, but though this may be stimulating, it can in itself never provide complete satisfaction. All students will inevitably reach a point in their studies when they will become disillusioned. The reason for this is because the more they learn, the more it heightens the awareness of their ignorance. In reality people do not know very much about anything.

Some people, however, will tell us that education can answer every problem. Their argument is: 'If we educate people about the dangers of … they won't do it.' How mistaken they are! It is a fact of life that clever people often do very stupid things, leading to tragic results. The warning not to do something is for many people a good reason to do it. Thus, we have to accept that education alone is not sufficient to keep a person from making bad choices. There are many problems which human ingenuity can never solve. Society today attaches great significance to intellect, learning and understanding which is, of course, commendable. People should continually strive to be educated to the best of their ability so that they are well equipped for life's work. But although it is desirable to be educated, and to realise that education is a lifetime pursuit, this route will fail to produce lasting contentment. Quite the contrary! To increase knowledge only increases sorrow; for the greater our knowledge, the more we realise that of itself it cannot unravel the mystery of human existence, nor satisfactorily explain the purpose of creation. The author of the book of Ecclesiastes clearly shows that the route of education was not the answer to his search for ultimate peace and happiness. That is because at the end of life it is of no use; it dies with us.

Enjoyment

The second route we might try is that of enjoyment. From the intellectual we can turn to the emotional, from the company of philosophers to that of playboys. It has long been believed that lasting happiness in this world depends on many different life circumstances. But can a person be happy by constantly entertaining themselves? What follows is a thought that many people have:

> I said to myself, 'Come now, I will test you with pleasure to find out what is good.' But that also proved to be meaningless. 'Laughter,' I said, 'is madness. And what does pleasure accomplish?' I tried cheering

12

myself with wine, and embracing folly – my mind still guiding me with wisdom. I wanted to see what was good for people to do under the heavens during the few days of their lives.[3]

What is important for us to remember is that his mind still guided him with wisdom. He did not launch himself into debauchery. Neither did he become a slave to any of these pursuits, as many people do. He knew that unrestrained indulgence would only lead to increased misery. Therefore, it was a carefully controlled experiment to try to discover the value of purely earthly pleasures.

Sadly there are many people today who are seeking happiness through drink or drugs and usually they are miserable because of rejection and fear. The modern picture of a heavy drinker being a tough person is a lie. These are not strong people. They are weak. Their reputation for being someone who lives life to the full does not in any way match reality.

Any addicted person is no longer in control of his or her life, but is invariably insecure. Some addicts cannot even accept that a problem exists. Alcoholics may rightfully say that they can go several days without touching alcohol, implying that they are in full control of their situation. Alcoholics, indeed those ruled by any habit, will often practise self-deceit and fail to realise the sad state that they have reached. Neither are they always aware of the tremendous grief and anguish that it can cause to their family and friends.

Only by being honest about an addiction can any progress be made, for you cannot deal with any problem until it is recognised. An Ethiopian proverb wisely says, 'He who conceals his disease cannot expect to be cured.' To acknowledge powerlessness and unmanageability for any form of addiction is the first step towards recovery.

'Eat, drink and be merry, for tomorrow we die' (see 1 Corinthians 15:32) is for some the complete purpose of life. But how wrong they are! Aldous Huxley had it exactly right when he wrote: 'Oh, how desperately bored, in spite of their grim determination to have a good time, the majority of pleasure seekers really are!'[4] Past experience repeatedly reveals that indulging in pleasures, whether crude or cultural, will not finally satisfy our deepest needs and may lead to disaster. How many people have turned to drink or drugs in an attempt to dull the emotional pains of life? How many have died prematurely because of the inability to keep their bodily appetites under control? Entertainment has its place, but it can only help us to escape the reality of life temporarily.

Those who appear to be the life and soul of the party are often the loneliest people present. It is perhaps hard to believe that someone who is making people laugh could be depressed. Laughter's the best medicine, right? There is an element of truth in that, but it does not provide a solution to every problem. A fact that we must come to terms with is that many clowns and comedians are depressed. The American actor and comedian Robin Williams had a career that many would envy. Yet on 11 August 2014, he committed suicide at his home in California at the age of sixty-three. A man who had brought joy to many millions very clearly experienced the depths of despair. Tony Hancock, another gifted actor and comedian, ended his own life on 24 June 1968 in Sydney. He read widely and avidly in an attempt to discover the meaning of life, but obviously to no avail, for death appeared to be the best option. Spike Milligan commented in 1989: 'Very difficult man to get on with. He used to drink excessively. You felt sorry for him. He ended up on his own. I thought, he's got rid of everybody else, he's going to get rid of himself and he did.'[5] Hancock and Williams are not unique in discovering that laughter alone does not produce real happiness and that death can appear to be the best option.

15

Employment

Some people try to find meaning and purpose for life through their pursuit of a career, and they will fail. The motivation may be to help others. Or it may be nothing more than selfish ambition. But whatever the driving force, work alone will not lead to total satisfaction. For, like anything else, the fact of death means that all we accumulate or achieve must be left behind.

Working, even just to survive, can be a very time-consuming process. And a further problem for many is that they work far more hours than they need. They may appear to be very successful, hard-working men or women, but in reality they are workaholics. Building their business or climbing the promotion ladder at work has taken full control of their lives. As a result, family responsibilities are neglected with dire consequences. It is difficult, if not impossible, to be married to someone who is married to their career rather than their partner. Any children will also suffer in such relationships because overwork and stress are great enemies of good parenting. Golda Meir, the fourth prime minister of Israel, admitted that she had nagging doubts about the price her children had paid for her career. She said, 'You can get used to anything if you have to, even to feeling perpetually guilty.'[6]

Enrichment

The final route is to create things that will last after death. It is the joy of creativity. A person may surround themselves with objects of splendour and luxury. He or she may build fine houses, create beautiful gardens, or amass treasures. But what does it amount to?

It is true that the route of enrichment may result in great satisfaction and sensual pleasure. Yet, in spite of that, it can never truly satisfy. The reason is, of course, that it has all been done before. There is nothing new under the sun. Remember, too, that our life on earth is a brief pilgrimage and all our possessions must be left behind. We brought absolutely nothing with us when we came into the world, and we can take nothing out of it when we leave. 'Naked I came from my mother's womb, and naked I shall depart', says Job.[7] Or to quote a Jewish proverb: 'There are no pockets in shrouds.'

The fact that we leave all our earthly possessions behind inevitably leads us to ask the urgent question: 'What will happen to our achievements and acquisitions when we are gone?' This was a major problem for the author of Ecclesiastes. He says, 'I hated all the things I had toiled for under the sun, because I must leave them to the one who comes after me. And who knows whether he will be a wise

17

man or a fool? Yet he will have control over all the work into which I have poured my effort and skill under the sun. This too is meaningless.'[8]

Dissatisfaction arises in the first instance because we have to leave these things for ever. But then the grief is accentuated by another consideration. That is, someone else will inherit them. Will it be a wise person or a fool? Irresponsibility or incompetence can see the work which we loved, and over which we laboured, be easily lost. Time will tell. And, if we have no successor, what is the point of acquisition? It all seems so meaningless, a chasing after the wind; nothing is gained under the sun.

Conclusion

The lesson from all of this should be obvious. It is that the search for satisfaction can be costly and lead to scepticism and despair because of the meaninglessness of it all. The author of the book of Ecclesiastes repeatedly likens it to chasing after the wind, which is a useless occupation. It is to snatch at something and catch nothing. What, then, should be our attitude to these various routes? The answer is that education, employment, enjoyment and enrichment when rightly used can be meaningful and pleasant. Be that as it may, there is a great danger that we try to get much more from them than they can ever give. These routes are never the solution to humanity's greatest problem, which is to understand the purpose of life. Thus we must continue on our journey of discovery.

A pause for thought

What is my ultimate goal in life? Will pursuing any goal solely for personal advancement result in total satisfaction? How do I support my answer?

A TIME FOR EVERYTHING

There is a time for everything, and a season for every activity under
the heavens:
a time to be born and a time to die,
a time to plant and a time to uproot,
a time to kill and a time to heal,
a time to tear down and a time to build,
a time to weep and a time to laugh,
a time to mourn and a time to dance,
a time to scatter stones and a time to gather them,
a time to embrace and a time to refrain from embracing,
a time to search and a time to give up,
a time to keep and a time to throw away,
a time to tear and a time to mend,
a time to be silent and a time to speak,
a time to love and a time to hate,
a time for war and a time for peace.

(Ecclesiastes 3:1–8)

TIME IS A VERY PRECIOUS THING because how we use
it determines the kind of people that we become
and the future that we have. The passing of time
escapes no one and once we have lost it we can never get

it back. Therefore, time needs to be handled with extreme care. It is sometimes said, 'better late than never', but usually never late is better.

The days, weeks, months and years of our lives pass by very quickly. Our time on earth is not just marching on, it is running out. As soon as we are born we begin to die, and that death can occur at any time, by disaster or disease, if not by the inevitable decline of old age. Thus, what we call 'the land of the living' could equally be called 'the land of the dying'. Perhaps before it is realised, our time can be gone. The Scottish poet Robert Burns had it exactly right when he wrote: 'Nae man can tether time or tide'.[1] The clock never stops ticking. Time is not under human control or arrangement and so it is impossible to cancel the inevitable; we are destined to die.

The English poet Robert Herrick also expresses this same thought in these words:

> Gather ye rosebuds while ye may,
> Old Time is still a-flying:
> And this same flower that smiles to-day,
> To-morrow will be dying.[2]

We have to accept the fact that there is a certain time for the birth and the death of every individual. So let us ask ourselves some urgent questions: 'What is achieved between our cradle and the grave?' 'Do we live life to the fullest?' 'Do we utilise our time wisely and responsibly, realising that death may be much nearer than we think?' 'Do we make the most of every opportunity however challenging, sometimes intimidating, it might be?' Or perhaps we are very busy achieving nothing? Maybe we have never addressed these questions, even though every one of us should do so as a matter of urgency.

Within Ecclesiastes 3 is a poem, the best known and most often quoted section of the book, in which the word 'time' is used on twenty-eight occasions. Fourteen contrasting pairs are employed which practically cover every major aspect of human life. The repetition of 'a time ... and a time ...' suggests that nothing we do has any permanence. We move from one situation to another, and back again. As a result, our moods continually change because of the situations in which we find ourselves. These may, or may not, be of our own making, but whatever the reasons, we are inevitably subject to the march of time and to change.

All of us, during our lifespan, will encounter momentous events which can change us for better or worse. Life will have its ups and downs; swinging from one extreme to another by the influence of forces we often do not control. A brief moment can result in a tremendous change. Upheavals such as an unexpected job loss, a severe illness, a tragic accident, the death of a loved one, a failed marriage, good fortune and so much more can swiftly affect our lives. There will be times of sadness and times of joy, times to weep and times to laugh.

Despite the fact that life is full of ups and downs – times when we weep and times when we laugh – it also reveals continuity. Everything in life, as we saw earlier, follows a pattern. Night is followed by day, and winter is followed by spring. Birth is followed by death, and war is followed by peace, and so the cycle continues. But why, we might ask, should these things happen? Is it because of chance or choice? In what follows we will look at some of the answers that have been given.

Many people are of the opinion that what happens to them in life is simply due to the arbitrary whim of chance – in other words, by luck. They just happen to be in the right place at the right time, or in the wrong place at the wrong time. Fortune or misfortune, they believe, is an occurrence without any discoverable cause. That is the way it is. But is it?

The alternative to chance is choice. There are those who will tell us that the choice is theirs and that they can do whatever they want. The English poet William Ernest Henley, who died in 1903, wrote, 'I am the master of my fate: I am the captain of my soul.'[3] Free will, independence and the ability to control our own destiny is one popular point of view. Then there are others who believe that their future is determined by those in positions of power and authority. As a consequence they have someone to blame when things go wrong. This is how many people react to anyone in a position of authority who doesn't see things their way.

Is it a matter of chance or choice that we exist? Is it possible that there is a superior being who created and controls the universe? There are those who tell us that if we look into the beauty of creation we must be able to see a creator. If not, we must be blind. But is this a reasonable comment? Can there be a God who reigns, who is in control, and who is not limited by the circumstances of time? And further, is it possible to answer these questions with any degree of certainty?

Who, or what, is it that causes the seasons for every activity? According to the Bible, it is very clear that God is in control. It also tells us that individuals have a degree of liberty. This can be explained by a very simple illustration. Imagine that it is winter. We may decide to stay in a warm house or venture out into the cold. The choice is ours; what is predestined is that winter comes. God is in sovereign control of it all and sets the times, but we are both accountable and responsible to use our time well.

Despite the preciousness of time, it is very easy for us to put things off until another day. Is that a wise or a foolish thing to do? Surely the fact that we should carefully consider is that we do not know what that day will bring. Jesus told a story which vividly illustrates the brevity and uncertainty of life. It was about a man who had a farm that produced excellent crops. So far as we know, there was nothing notably immoral about his conduct. He was probably a hard-working man who had become wealthy because of his diligence. But full of confidence he arrogantly said, 'I will pull down my barns and build bigger ones. Then I will have sufficient space to store everything. There will be enough stored away for years to come. And I will take life easy; eat, drink and be merry.' But God said to him, 'You fool! You will die this very night.'[4] The truth was that his desire was founded on an illusion. It was founded on the desire for security, but his wealth provided him with no security at all. This man was foolish not because he was rich or successful; such things can be a great blessing. His fatal mistake was because he failed to realise that he could not determine the length of his life and the route it would take. Some things were within his control whilst others were not. As we are all only too aware, life is full of surprises.

King Solomon concluded that life is anything but monotonous, for we have no idea what problems may challenge us at any given time. No wonder he wrote, 'Do not boast about tomorrow, for you do not know what a day may bring.'[5] None of us can write in our diaries with any certainty what we shall do tomorrow, much less next year. What a difference a day can make! Obviously planning for our future is sensible and necessary, but we should always guard against presumptuousness. Factors unknown to us might intervene at any time so that our plans do not materialise. That is why a proper perspective on the fleeting nature and unpredictability of this earthly life should teach us to do all that we can, while we can.

Time should always be utilised to the fullest advantage. But, having said that, the most common and easiest answer when confronted with a challenge is to say, 'I will do it some other time.' It is often said that finding time is the problem. 'Yes, I am interested. Yes, I should like to do it. Unfortunately, it is impossible at present because I am far too busy doing other things.' Those who speak like this will probably be saying the same thing throughout their lives. The time will never be right and nothing will ever be achieved. Therefore, do not delay in doing something that should be done now. Live for today because yesterday is gone and tomorrow might never come. I suggest that you think very carefully about this before proceeding to the next stage of our journey.

A pause for thought

It is important that we have a proper perspective on the fleeting nature of this earthly life. Then we shall use our time responsibly and make the most of every opportunity. That is not to say we fill every moment with activities or try to do everything that comes our way. Part of our day should be allocated to relaxation and sleep.

Understanding when, where and how to use time involves being able to discern what should be done and what can be set aside. List your priorities. How much time do you allocate to each? Are you allocating the correct amount of time to each of them according to their value? Why or why not?

LIFE'S NOT FAIR

And I saw something else under the sun: in the place of judgement – wickedness was there, in the place of justice – wickedness was there.

(Ecclesiastes 3:16)

Again I looked and saw all the oppression that was taking place under the sun: I saw the tears of the oppressed – and they have no comforter; power was on the side of their oppressors – and they have no comforter.

(Ecclesiastes 4:1)

There is something else meaningless that occurs on earth: the righteous who get what the wicked deserve, and the wicked who get what the righteous deserve. This too, I say, is meaningless.

(Ecclesiastes 8:14)

HOW OFTEN HAVE YOU HEARD a child use the phrase, 'It's not fair'? Children are exceptionally quick to observe if someone is treated better than themselves, and they will usually not hesitate to complain. 'It's not fair that they have got more than me!' they say, and sometimes the difference can be very small.

It is occasionally said that if you wish to share something like an apple between two children you should let one cut it and the other have first choice. Then you will get two pieces which are exactly equal and there will be no argument.

'It is not fair' is an attitude adopted by people from their earliest years and normally it develops throughout life. No matter what our age, we do not like to see injustice. As we grow older we become more adept and tend to use language which is much more sophisticated and subtler than that of children, but basically we are saying the same thing. I should be paid more for my work. I should have been promoted. I deserve to be treated better. These are just a few of the alternative ways of saying, 'It's not fair.'

Many situations in life shout, 'It's not fair!' This attitude is well illustrated by a story Jesus told about some workers in a vineyard.[1] A landowner goes out early one morning to hire workers. When he has agreed with them on a daily wage, he sends them into his vineyard. At around nine o'clock in the morning he hires more men, even though the day is partly gone. These workers have no right to claim a full day's wage, but the landowner promises to pay them whatever is right at the end of the day. Around noon and then again around three in the afternoon he does the same thing. Payment is not mentioned. Then, at about five o'clock, he goes out and hires more men. By now the workday is almost complete. That evening, the owner of the vineyard tells his foreman to call the workers in and pay them, beginning with the last workers first. They are paid the same wage that has been promised to the men hired early in the morning. When those hired earlier come to get their pay, they think they will receive more than what they have agreed on earlier in the day. But they, too, are paid the same amount. Of course, they complain! They feel cheated, even though they have received a fair day's pay for a fair day's work.

If you were to read this story to an employer, to a trade union representative or a worker, their most likely reaction would be, 'It is not fair.' It would be considered to be idealistic, impractical and a certain formula for disaster. To pay everyone the same irrespective of the work done and to pay first those who had done least work appears to be contrary to reason. The landowner appears to have been unfair and the immediate normal reaction would be to sympathise with the grumblers. Surely it is not fair that a man who has worked twelve hours, and especially in the hot climate of the Middle East, should be paid the same as someone who has worked for only one hour in the cool of the day? Do not those who do most deserve to be paid more? What is the incentive to work hard if everyone receives the same reward? Does not the landowner create bitterness in others by being unfair? Or is there more here than at first meets the eye?

Looking at this story from another perspective reveals a totally different picture. Instead of being about a man who is less than fair, it is about a man who is more than fair. Hence, when the grumbling occurred the landowner could rightly say, 'The cause of the bad relationship is not in my action but in your attitude.' The owner had fulfilled his agreement with them and they would have been satisfied had they not seen that others were getting a better deal than themselves. They really had no genuine reason to complain. Their dissatisfaction was a result of their jealousy and greed, alongside their failure to be satisfied with what they had agreed as a rightful wage for their labour. These are very common traits which make people oblivious to the needs of others and cause them to be self-centred.

Associated with the phrase 'it is not fair' are unhealthy emotions such as anger, bitterness, envy, jealousy, pride and resentment, to name but a few. These are bad for people, even physically, for to constantly live with them will eventually result in bad health. But that is not all. Such unhealthy attitudes result in comparisons being made with other people, and instead of loving them they will be hated.

Generally people refer to something being unfair when they compare themselves to those who are better off. It is much rarer for them to be anxious for those who are worse off because by nature people envy those above them. We have matured greatly in character when we are angrier about the suffering of others rather than our own. This should challenge us to ask ourselves some serious questions here. For instance: 'Do I love my neighbour as myself?' 'Am I oblivious to the needs of those who are poor and oppressed?' 'Am I prepared to work for justice and fairness for others?'

Injustice has been found in the most unlikely places. But it is especially difficult to accept when it appears in situations such as courts of law where we would expect justice. This is a problem which perplexed a prophet called Habakkuk when he saw the extreme wickedness, disregard for the law and injustice in Judah and Jerusalem, and the rising power of wicked Babylon. It is easy to understand why Habakkuk was completely confused and why he complained to his God.

How long, LORD, must I call for help, but you do not listen? Or cry out to you, 'Violence!' but you do not save? Why do you make me look at injustice? Why do you tolerate wrongdoing? Destruction and violence are before me; there is strife, and conflict abounds. Therefore the law is paralysed, and justice never prevails. The wicked hem in the righteous, so that justice is perverted.[2]

How could a good and just God who is in control of everything allow such terrible things to happen? That is the problem facing Habakkuk, and many others since. So what is the truth about God? Indeed, is there a God? Is there anybody in control of our universe, considering that the distribution and degree of suffering appear to be entirely random? Can the fact that there is so much evil and suffering in the world be satisfactorily reconciled with an all-powerful God of love and justice? Here we come face to face with questions that no serious thinking person can truthfully avoid.

There are two things which are wrong for any judge or jury to do. The first is to condemn the innocent and the second is to acquit the guilty. The French essayist and moralist, Joseph Joubert rightly said, 'Justice is truth in action.'[3] The sad fact is that justice does not always prevail. The words of a proverb rightly say, 'Laws, like the spider's web, catch the fly and let the hawks go free.'

The judicial system can be corrupted just like anything else. History merely repeats itself. It has all been done before. For instance, the arrest of Jesus was as a result of a bribe, namely: thirty silver coins which the traitorous Judas received from the chief priests.[4] Not only that! We are told that the 'chief priests and the whole Sanhedrin were looking for false evidence against Jesus so that they could put him to death'.[5] In reality, the whole trial was corrupt. It was the premeditated murder of an innocent man.

Injustice and bribery happened in the past and it happens now. In some countries political skulduggery, oppressive bureaucracy, financial corruption, exploitation and domination of the poor are a way of life. People in positions of power who have a responsibility to set a good example sometimes do not make good use of it. A further aspect is that their behaviour can easily influence those they come into contact with, making them bad too. As someone has said, 'Corruption is like a ball of snow: whence once set a-rolling it must increase.'[6] That is why we see injustice and cruelty in our world. It is not at all surprising that we regularly hear about monstrous levels of child abuse and of lives ruined by those who abuse their power. This is what it is really like.

Being caught up in a web of oppression and exploitation can lead a person to say, 'The dead are better off than the living. And most fortunate of all are those who were never born.' What made the situation of these sufferers so desperate was that there is no one under the sun who can comfort them. The oppressors possess the power and so their victims are helpless to seek any redress against earthly injustice. Such constant oppression and a sense of despair rob people of their energy and a desire for life. The ideal that they strive for and the reality they see within and around them are so far apart that the situation appears to be hopeless.

We should never underestimate the power of depression! It is so powerful that even several prominent biblical characters became discouraged with life to such a degree that they either wanted to die or desired that they had never been born.[7] It is for this kind of reason that people say, 'Life's not fair!' We see evidence of this throughout our lives. There is no escaping the fact that good people are often made to suffer while the wicked may prosper. Good people are sometimes treated as though they were wicked, and wicked people are sometimes treated as though they were good.

Why does crime frequently pay, and sometimes very well? This is a question that is often asked, for anyone with an observant eye will see oppression and social injustice. It is an obvious fact that people do not necessarily receive the reward or retribution of their deeds in this life. Hence, our knowledge of life 'under the sun' raises several major issues that perhaps need to be considered from a different perspective. For this reason we need to continue our journey so as to try to find satisfactory answers to life's many major difficulties and perplexities.

A pause for thought

Built into our nature is an internal judicial system; the conscience. It provides us with a moral sense of whether we are doing right or wrong. But this regulator of justice does not say the same thing to everyone. As a result we will react to our fellow human beings in different ways. Are you ever guided by selfish ambition? Or do you always desire to do what is good and not harmful to others? What implications does this have for you?

THE RAT RACE

And I saw that all toil and all achievement spring from one person's envy of another. This too is meaningless, a chasing after the wind.
Fools fold their hands and ruin themselves.
Better one handful with tranquillity
than two handfuls with toil
and chasing after the wind.
Again I saw something meaningless under the sun:
there was a man all alone;
he had neither son nor brother.
There was no end to his toil,
yet his eyes were not content with his wealth.
'For whom am I toiling' he asked,
'and why am I depriving myself of enjoyment?'
This too is meaningless –
a miserable business!

(Ecclesiastes 4:4–8)

SOME MEMBERS OF THE ANIMAL KINGDOM are cooperative with each other. They work together as a team and accomplish feats that would be impossible for an individual. Familiar examples of this are social insects such as termites, ants and various species of bees and wasps.

Animals often work as a group for their common good. Emperor penguins huddle together in large groups so as to survive the Antarctic winter. They cooperate by taking turns to occupy the coldest and warmest positions in the huddle. Groups of animals may be more successful in obtaining food than an individual. That is why lions will often hunt together when seeking large prey such as wildebeests. Living in a group can also provide protection. For instance, one baboon may fail to fight off a leopard whereas a troop of baboons is more able to do so.

On the other hand, there are some animals which do not cooperate and will even attack their own species. Such an example is the rat. For this reason the words 'rat race' are often used to describe a fiercely competitive struggle for position or power – a situation in which the law of the jungle gains mastery or control. The philosopher and social scientist Herbert Spencer and later the naturalist Charles Darwin described it as the survival of the fittest.

Today tremendous emphasis is placed upon speed and success, regardless of the consequences. Comparison and competition with our neighbours can be an extremely challenging and tiresome affair. It is the rat race, and the predominant reason for taking part is envy. People may desire what they do not have and envy the success others apparently seem to be enjoying. The self-centredness of envy is responsible for a person joining the rat race, and addiction keeps them there because the more they have the more they want. If left unchecked, possessiveness will inevitably lead to bitterness and conflict. It is a vicious circle from which there appears to be no easy escape. The German-born American psychoanalyst and philosopher, Erich Fromm aptly described it as 'a bottomless pit which exhausts the person in an endless effort to satisfy the need without ever reaching satisfaction'.[1]

Society is generally geared to achievement and speed. As a result, the constant pressures of modern life will sometimes lead to serious consequences. Of course, we should remember that individuals will react differently to these pressures. Some will achieve great success while others fail to keep up with the accelerating pace of life and will either give up or, if they ignore their limitations, suffer a nervous breakdown. Problems caused by stress increasingly affect the society in which we live and may even lead to suicide.

People sometimes argue that they are unable to afford to take time off because they have so much to do. Does that sound familiar? The truth is they often can't afford not to!

Regular periods of rest are a necessary part of a successful life. Live simply is the antidote to many of our problems.

We live in a world where we are constantly bombarded with incredible change from every direction. Life is becoming more and more complex and less and less secure. It is therefore not surprising that some people are deeply challenged to carefully reassess their situation. You may have heard someone say, 'I have too little time to appreciate and enjoy life.' Or, 'I want to spend more quality time with family and close friends.' It is often a yearning to escape from the rat race of extreme materialism to a much simpler lifestyle. How many people today are buying things they don't want, with money they don't have, to impress people they don't like? It is utterly meaningless, like chasing the wind.

We should regularly ask ourselves: 'How is it possible to cope in a world of rapid change and uncertainty? This is a question where we come face-to-face with reality. And if we are serious about this journey we shall at this point be compelled to take an honest look at the way we live. People who never find themselves asking, 'Why?' are obviously not thinking seriously. You and I must decide what our priority in life is if we are to make any significant progress. Is our number one priority a craving to earn more at every opportunity and to covet what others have; or is it to focus on relationships and other important values?

Some people make sweeping changes to their lifestyle because they believe that they are missing out on life. For instance, an ever-increasing number are 'downshifting' to improve the balance between work and leisure. In other words, it is an attempt to balance our need for an income with our desire to live life to the fullest. This can be achieved in various ways. People may move from the city and escape to the country so as to experience a less hectic pace of life. The high property prices in certain locations have encouraged some to sell and move to much cheaper areas. This may enable them to adopt a more comfortable lifestyle by providing a quieter and more spacious environment. But that is not all. A financial gain on their property sale may also allow them to take a lower paid, less stressful job, or even early retirement.

In reality, most people are unable to swap their homes for freeholdings in the countryside where they assume they will live happily ever after. The good news, however, is that there are alternative ways to reduce the problems that are making our lives more stressful. It may be possible to reduce our working week by avoiding various unnecessary expenses. Do we really need everything we have?

Throughout life we tend to accumulate many superfluous items which can be a liability by requiring constant cleaning and storage. Bookshelves may be filled with books that are never read. Do we need them? Wardrobes and drawers may be filled with clothes that are never worn. Do we need them? The answer in most instances is probably 'No', and for this reason many people favour a minimalist form of living. They retain things which are absolutely essential for a comfortable existence and eliminate what is left. This raises a crucial question at this stage of our journey: 'What should we do to achieve true satisfaction?' Surely it appears logical that getting rid of clutter in every area of our life can be a positive step, leading to a more simplified, practical and enjoyable lifestyle.

There are a few people who go much further and cease to participate in a race, a course of study, or in conventional society. They eagerly embrace a carefree lifestyle and take great pride in not being in the rat race. But here there is a major problem. 'The fool folds his hands and ruins himself.' This was a customary saying portraying, what we would call today, the 'dropout'. In his book of Proverbs, Solomon uses the term 'folding of the hands' to warn against the foolishness of indolence.[2] The great danger for the dropout is that he or she lose all grasp of reality and any desire and ambition to achieve anything in life. Anyone who abandons all ambitions and hopes for the future commits suicide in the sense that they destroy their self-respect.

The author of the book of Ecclesiastes considers two extreme attitudes which he believes are both meaningless. Firstly, someone may achieve things by toil, though unfortunately the motivating force is often nothing more than rivalry and envy. It is to be caught in the rat race of life. The opposite and equal error to this is to accept an attitude of laziness which produces no worthwhile achievements and ultimately leads to ruin. Hence, what should we do? The answer to the problem lies between the two. 'Better one handful with tranquillity than two handfuls with toil and chasing after the wind.' This is a picture of someone who does not participate in the rat race, nor try to escape from the usual responsibilities of life. Blessed are the balanced!

A major characteristic of a truly successful life will be cooperation instead of competition that is fuelled by pride; contentment instead of covetousness, and togetherness instead of loneliness. An obsession with wealth or personal advancement excludes all advantageous associations with others and so there will be no one to help in times of need. To be consumed by work to such an extent that it is impossible to establish close relationships is a serious mistake. Therefore on another stage of our journey we will together explore the advantages of companionship.

A pause for thought

It is an illusion to believe that the continual desire for more will lead to contentment. Instead, it will ultimately lead to dissatisfaction and a failure to achieve anything worthwhile. We cannot say that ambition is wrong of itself; it can be a helpful thing. But if we attempt to only advance our own reputation or cause it will create major problems. That is why in his letter to the Philippian Christians, Paul says to them (and us), 'Do nothing out of selfish ambition or vain conceit. Rather, in humility value others above yourselves, not looking to your own interests but each of you to the interests of the others.'[3] Excessive unhealthy competitiveness inevitably results in strife and prevents any worthwhile companionship.

6

THE LOVE OF MONEY

Whoever loves money never has money enough;
whoever loves wealth is never satisfied with their income. This too
is meaningless.

(Ecclesiastes 5:10)

HAVE YOU SEEN THE T-SHIRT that says, 'Money is not everything. There is also Visa, MasterCard and American Express'? It is a humorous and insightful picture of the modern way of life. There is something about money which is very special. It plays an essential role in our everyday lives and it will certainly influence the way we behave in varying degrees for better or for worse. How do we respond? Are we generous because we realise that the possessions we have are not what is most important? Or do we selfishly take for ourselves what is needed by others? What is a proper perspective towards money?

Tevye, the poor Jewish milkman who was the principal character in the musical *Fiddler on the Roof,* sang the song, 'If

I Were a Rich Man'. Have you, like Tevye, ever thought about what it would be like to be rich? Probably from time to time many of us daydream about possessing a vast sum of money and, moreover, what we would do with it. Perhaps we would give some of it to those in extreme need. Maybe we would buy expensive gifts for our family and friends, and luxuries for ourselves. But would this successfully fill a void in our lives by satisfying our deepest needs?

It has frequently been suggested that if people are rich they will be content. Of course, we need to look at the whole picture. Then we will see, with the teacher in Ecclesiastes, that in reality this is not necessarily so. The fact that we must come to terms with is that money and the things it can buy are not the answer to all our problems. Material things alone are never able to provide lasting satisfaction and a real sense of security.

To relate happiness to prosperity and hardship to poverty is a false assumption. It is very clear to any observant eye that true happiness bears no relationship whatever to a person's bank balance. The American billionaire Howard Hughes lived a glamorous life. He dated actresses, piloted aircraft, owned hotels around the world and even an airline to carry him on global jaunts. Yet, despite his immense wealth, he ended his life as a recluse and is remembered primarily because of the courtroom battles for his money. At the time of his death in 1976, after years of neglect, his body was almost unrecognisable. Barbara Hutton, heiress to the Woolworth fortune and one of the wealthiest women in the world, spent most of her life being made unhappy by men who were more interested in her money than in her.

These people are not unique, for history repeatedly reveals that vast wealth does not automatically result in happiness. Quite the contrary! As useful as money is, it has numerous limitations. It cannot buy us any of the things which make life truly worth living. For instance, it cannot buy us real love, or personality, or health, or immortality. Those who are rich may be abject failures, whilst those who are financially poor may be great masters at the art of living.

It is always wise to remember that our perspective on life is much more important than worldly possessions. The oil magnate and the first American worth more than a billion dollars, John D. Rockefeller gave a brilliant illustration of this when he said, 'The poorest man I know is the man who has got nothing but money.' How slow are people to learn this lesson! It is a well-known fact that amassing more and more things, whatever the amount, can never provide lasting happiness that always satisfies. Sometimes wealth can create far more problems than it solves.

A major disadvantage of wealth is that it can cause constant anxiety and sleeplessness. 'The sleep of a labourer is sweet, whether he eats little or much, but the abundance of a rich man permits him no sleep.'[1] This great truth led Roland Murphy to say, 'It seems as if the riches that the eyes contemplated so avidly now keep them from being closed in sleep.'[2] This is a major symptom of covetousness. On one hand, the poor have little to lose and therefore have less fear of loss. On the other hand, many of those who have a lot to lose will be obsessed by the risk of their loss and will experience sleepless nights and anxious days.

Someone has designed a safety bed which it is said will protect you against natural disasters, terrorist attacks, kidnappers and thieves. When a motion sensor detects a threat, it automatically surrounds its occupant with a bulletproof canopy. It can be fitted with optional features such as a CD player, a DVD player, a microwave and a refrigerator. You breathe filtered oxygen, use the available features, and wait comfortably in safety until any threat is removed. Even so, I am sure that not even an armour-protected bed can for some people guarantee a good night's sleep.

Wealth can easily be lost because it is void of stability. Circumstances may suddenly change and a fortune can disappear overnight, as it did for many when the world stock markets crashed in late October 1987. This was nothing new. It has all happened before. The catastrophic collapse of stock market prices on the New York Stock Exchange in October 1929 saw many banks forced into insolvency and thousands of individual investors ruined. This resulted in the Great Depression, which lasted for almost ten years; the longest ever experienced by the Western industrialised world. Again this was nothing new. In seventeenth-century Holland there was a speculative frenzy called 'Tulip Mania'. Prices for bulbs rose to unwarranted levels until February 1637. Then serious doubts were raised about whether prices could continue to increase. As a result, prices fell precipitately. Many investors lost money and a few faced financial ruin.

There are other instances similar to those above which could be quoted to stress that there is nothing new under the sun. Periods of boom and bust are a feature of history. Indeed, is it not inevitable that a combination of 'greed' and the 'herd instinct' will create a recipe for an excessive rise that will be followed by a dramatic crash? Why, then, do many people so often ignore the important lessons of history?

Any financial investment involves a degree of risk. Markets can be volatile and go down as well as up. That is why there are numerous reminders that past performance does not guarantee future gains. There are people who have bought property and then found themselves in positions of negative equity, and may be faced with repossession. Pension schemes have collapsed and businesses have failed. These examples reveal that financial investments are unstable and that the richest people in the world today can be poor tomorrow whether by misguided ventures, or because of factors beyond their control.

Some people believe that money is the root of all evil, but this is certainly not the case. According to the Bible, it is not money that is the problem. Having money is a tremendous privilege, as long as we use it wisely. Money is not a root of all kinds of evil; the *love* of it is.[3]

What, then, are the evils of which the love of money is a cause? Such a list would be very long. It would include judges who have perverted the cause of justice for bribes. 'When money speaks, the truth is often silent', as the saying goes. Politicians have accepted gifts in exchange for favours, or have claimed dubious expenses. Spies have sold their country's secrets to the enemy. Assassins are prepared to bargain over somebody's life. Business people have entered into illegal transactions to have their products promoted. Even so-called spiritual leaders have been known to commercialise religion. In the past there was the unscriptural and superstitious sale of indulgences. Today there are preachers and evangelists who appeal for money which is never publicly audited. The love of money has frequently been the cause of lies, thefts, frauds, murders and wars. It is the love of money which causes many shops to be open seven days in the week. Almost 'everybody has his or her price', the cynic will say.

Money can be like a drug, in that the more we have the more we need. Whereas hunger is satisfied with food, and thirst with drink, those with a hunger or thirst for wealth are never satisfied. For this reason covetous people are never content because the more they have, the more they want. It is a bitter cycle that never has a satisfying outcome. Such people are always dissatisfied with their present possessions. Similarly, misers are always miserable because their addiction results in them becoming a slave to their possessions. Greed is, in fact, idolatry. Not only that; such people are fools because they worship something which cannot be kept.

How absurd it is to believe that wealth by itself brings true happiness! Furthermore, to have money and not be able to enjoy it must be one of the most futile and frustrating experiences in life. Some of the wealthiest people in the world are also some of the most miserable because their lives are so incredibly empty. Even worse than the addiction money brings, is the emptiness it leaves. The American pastor and prolific writer Warren Wiersbe captured what this means when he wrote, 'Why does a person eat? So that he can add years to his life. But what good is it for me to add years to my life *if I don't add life to my years?*'[4]

To become obsessed with the love of wealth is a serious mistake. Neither, it should be said, is there any great virtue in being poor, or having to struggle to survive. We all need to buy food, clothing and shelter for ourselves and our families. That is a fact of life. The important point to remember, however, is that money and possessions do not by themselves ultimately satisfy. True happiness always comes from personal relationships, as we shall see on another stage of our journey. Meanwhile, let us remember that money is neither good nor bad; it all depends on how we obtain it and what we do with it.

John Wesley, the great eighteenth-century preacher and founder of the Methodist Church, stated precisely what our attitude towards wealth ought to be when he said,

'Earn all you can, save all you can, give all you can.' This lesson is specially needed today because we live in a society that is primarily preoccupied with getting rather than giving. Therefore, the vast majority fail to experience personally the truth of Christ's saying, 'It is more blessed to give than to receive.'[5] That is sound advice that can lead us to a new and joyful life.

Neither the possession nor the retention of money or worldly things is wrong in itself, providing we obtain them honestly and keep them with a justifiable motive. The vital question is: 'Who is in charge?' Are our possessions controlling us, or are we controlling our possessions? If we discover there is some material possession that we cannot live without, we should give it away. Undoubtedly our freedom depends upon it.

A pause for thought

We need to be careful in our borrowing so as to avoid becoming slaves to debt. Neither should we accumulate excessive wealth. It isn't what we have or don't have that leads to generosity and happiness. Some people with very limited financial resources are exceptionally generous in their giving to religious or charitable causes, irrespective of their own present needs or future requirements. Of course, poverty does not necessarily create unselfishness, just as wealth does not necessarily result in giving. Whatever our position, money can become addictive and eventually take full control of our life.

The way to avoid becoming a slave to money is consistent and spontaneous sacrificial giving to those whose needs are real. And when we see what our giving does in the lives of others, it rewards us in a way that the retention of money and personal possessions never can. We do well to remember that it is foolish to set one's hopes on what can so easily be lost.

7

LONELINESS OR COMPANIONSHIP

Two are better than one,
because they have a good return for their labour:
if either of them falls down,
one can help the other up.
But pity anyone who falls
and has no one to help them up.
Also, if two lie down together, they will keep warm.
But how can one keep warm alone?
Though one may be overpowered,
two can defend themselves.
A cord of three strands is not quickly broken.

(Ecclesiastes 4:9–12)

WE LIVE IN A WORLD in which some people try to detach themselves from others. But that, I believe, is a serious mistake. God said in Genesis, 'It is not good for the man to be alone. I will make a helper suitable for him.'[1] Since then there has been a general recognition that we need to love and be loved. Human beings are fundamentally social creatures, and as such are dependent upon one another in many different ways. It cannot be too strongly emphasised that loneliness is a major contributor to mental and physical illness in our society. Therefore, it is important to remember that all of us need to develop healthy relationships here on earth if we are ever to experience true success and real happiness. To be constantly alone, without the support of family and close friends, is a pitiful state to be in.

At the outset of this stage of our journey we should realise that loneliness is not necessarily the same as being alone. We may feel lonely, isolated and vulnerable while alone, but it is also possible to experience these feelings in a crowd, or even in a family or a marriage. Loneliness is not necessarily greatly helped by a busy social life or the number of people with whom we make contact, but instead it is dependent on our relationship to those people.

Freddie Mercury, the flamboyant vocalist and gifted lyricist of the rock band Queen, said in an interview:

> Because audiences love me, it's hard for them to believe that somebody like Freddie Mercury could be lonely …In fact, my kind of loneliness is the hardest. I can be in a crowd and still be the loneliest person, because I don't really belong to anyone. Over the years I have become bitter and I don't trust anybody because they've let me down so many times. The more you are let down, the more you are hurt.[2]

The more you are hurt, the more difficult it is to make friends and develop meaningful relationships. Thus the unbroken sequence of reciprocal cause and effect creates a vicious circle.

To be alone is to be by oneself, and that is often essential to provide respite from a busy life. Now, more than ever, people need regular periods of solitude. Being alone, but not lonely, enables them to reflect on their past and deliberate on their future. This journey of reflection may not always be a comfortable and pretty one. But on the whole it should be helpful. Solitude allows people to concentrate on what is vital for their well-being, and it should also allow them to be in a better position to fulfil the tasks before them. That is why many people wisely choose to spend time alone, as Jesus did, in solitude, meditation and prayer.[3]

On the other hand, to be really lonely is to experience the unpleasant feelings of abandonment. It is to desperately want meaningful social contact and yet apparently be unable to achieve it. This condition may be short-term or long-term. Short-term loneliness is the result of immediate circumstances, for example the death of a loved one, the breakdown of an important relationship, or the temporary isolation from our usual circle of friends and family through moving to another area. In contrast, long-term loneliness is not necessarily linked to present circumstances. It has roots which are firmly based in the personality or past experiences of the individual. Such people will inevitably find it very difficult, maybe impossible, to develop any happy and fulfilling relationships with others wherever they are.

Some people are driven by loneliness to do things they would not normally do. They may resort to drink, take drugs or become a slave to work in an attempt to satisfy their needs. King Saul tried to overcome his problems by listening to David's music.[4] He began his reign successfully, but ended it as a deeply lonely and terrified man, struggling in vain to control his future.[5] Because of his rebelliousness and unwillingness to seek correct guidance, he ruined his life. He was not unique. There are many people today who do nothing about their loneliness. They accept it as a way of life and therefore make no attempt to develop any meaningful relationships. That is a serious mistake because loneliness avoided does not go away. So how, then, do we make friends and conquer loneliness?

There are those who obviously need the help of a counsellor to overcome their chronic sense of loneliness. In many situations, however, it is possible to tackle this problem without such help. People can begin by asking what the reasons that prevent them from having friends are. Maybe it is nothing more than shyness or an inability to communicate. Perhaps it is because of the belief that they have nothing to contribute to a relationship and therefore fear that any friendship will not last. They might encounter difficulty in trusting people or dread the consequences of a wrong relationship. Despite such obstacles, it is essential to have a purpose in life; something to give people the sense that their existence is meaningful. Hence, any who are lonely should not wait for someone to call, or to write, or to visit them. That might never happen. Instead, they should take the initiative and *be* a friend.

This raises the urgent question: 'How does one discover true friends?' There are many people who will say, 'He's a good friend of mine,' but in reality this is often a gross exaggeration. There is a vast difference between having friendly feelings towards someone and true friendship. For this reason we need to recognise the major characteristic of true friendship if we are ever going to make any progress. A familiar proverb says, 'A friend in need is a friend indeed' and this is a wise observation. It is a fact that an ideal friendship continues regardless of changing external circumstances. An ideal friend will stand by you even when everyone else opposes or ignores you.

Without close friendship I would suggest that life is extremely bleak. We all need to have at least one person, and preferably several, whom we can trust and share our deepest needs with. Of course, it is important to note that in any marriage or close friendship there is a price to be paid. A mutually advantageous relationship always involves giving and taking and not one partner exploiting another. Even so, there is no doubt in my mind that the benefits of a true friendship far outweigh the cost of a person's independence.

The author of Ecclesiastes draws our attention to several important advantages of companionship. For instance, he reminds us that two people can accomplish more than twice as much as one. When people work together they divide the effort and multiply the effect. Sometimes a person cannot do a job alone, for it needs another pair of hands. A Jewish proverb aptly reminds us that 'A friendless man is like the left hand without the right'.

Friendship also allows people to bear one another's burdens. If one person falls, the other can reach out and help. But people who are alone when they fall have no faithful friend who is ready to help them up. This truth is not only applicable to actual falls which occur physically, but also to any setbacks that might be encountered. That being the case, we are very much dependent upon one another.

Then we come to the warmth of human relationships. This could be seen as a reference to marriage, but it should also be remembered that travellers in the days in which Ecclesiastes was written often slept together on a cold night so as to gain warmth from each other. How could one be warm alone? The very old King David slept with the virgin Abishag because no matter how many blankets covered him, he could not keep warm.[6]

Another major benefit of companionship is that of protection against a physical attack. If an enemy finds a person alone, that person is much more likely to be defeated. But with the help of another, it will either deter or make it much easier to withstand an attack. The reference to a 'cord of three strands' emphasises the strength of unity. Or, to quote an Ethiopian proverb: 'When spider webs unite, they can tie up a lion.' To sum it all up, worthwhile associations are far superior and safer than solitary selfishness.

Jesus told a story about a shrewd manager.[7] This manager was accused of squandering or wasting his employer's possessions. It may have been due to mismanagement rather than fraud or embezzlement. Whatever the reason, he faced certain dismissal. He had a very big problem. He also, realising that his situation was desperate, thought of a crafty scheme to ensure his future well-being. One by one he called in his master's debtors and substantially reduced their debts. It was a shrewd move, because the debtors were now indebted to him. Thus they would not refuse him help and hospitality after he lost his position as manager.

At this point an important question arises: 'What will be the master's reaction when he receives the account books?' He soon realises, of course, what has happened, and this is where the story takes an unexpected turn. The master, instead of admonishing his dishonest manager, admired him because he had acted shrewdly. What is this saying to us? 'Surely, no respectable person would condone such behaviour!' Even so, that is what the master did, and Jesus agreed with him. He admired him not because he had been dishonest, but because he had planned ahead and made provision for his future needs. As we shall see later, a wise person is one who can see beyond the present situation and be prepared for the future.

A pause for thought

Does relaxing and working with others play an important part in my life, or do I tend to go it alone? What implications does this have for me? Have I prepared for my future needs in a wise and careful way? Why or why not?

8

A POSITION OF POWER

Better a poor but wise youth than an old but foolish king who no longer knows how to heed a warning. The youth may have come from prison to the kingship, or he may have been born in poverty within his kingdom. I saw that all who lived and walked under the sun followed the youth, the king's successor. There was no end to all the people who were before them. But those who came later were not pleased with the successor. This too is meaningless, a chasing after the wind.

(Ecclesiastes 4:13–16).

S IR JOHN EMERICH EDWARD DALBERG-ACTON, first Baron Acton, in a letter to Mandell Creighton wrote the often quoted words: 'Power tends to corrupt, and absolute power corrupts absolutely.' In sharp contrast an anonymous source has said, 'Power can corrupt, but absolute power is absolutely delightful.' When challenging these opinions it is easy to overstep the mark and, as a result, reach wrong conclusions. What is certain is that the possession of power can change people for better or for worse.

It is of interest to note that the possession of power creates many problems which would not otherwise be encountered. Also, contrary to what we might expect, reaching the pinnacle of power does not inevitably result in fulfilment. It can never provide true satisfaction to those who make it the primary object of their endeavours. This is because all that lies ahead of them is stagnation and extinction. Probably some people will consider this to be a cynical or defeatist attitude, especially those who are rapidly climbing the so-called ladder of success, but it is a fact. In the words of Thomas Gray's (1716–71) well-known elegy: 'The paths of glory lead but to the grave.'

We might achieve great power and authority, but in a very short period of time it can all be swept away. For this reason, important questions that we should ask ourselves are: 'What do people get for all their hard work?' and 'What is the meaning and purpose of life under the sun?' People live, and people die, but nothing really changes.

Seeking a position of power can be very costly in terms of time, effort, money and the ability to maintain high moral standards. Family and friends may have to be neglected and enjoyments sacrificed through lack of time. Those seeking power may be financially rich and rapidly climbing the ladder of success, but their home could be unhappy. This, perhaps, would be despite giving their children or partner numerous presents to compensate for his or her absence. And we must seriously question that. Gifts are always an inadequate substitute for the giving of ourselves. It is impossible to ever buy true love. Children need parents, wives need husbands and vice versa. Healthy relationships, as we saw in the previous chapter, are always a central element of true success and should never be neglected.

Some people, in their ceaseless pursuit of money and power, will do whatever is necessary to achieve their selfish goal. Not only are family and friends overlooked; these people are also willing to lie and cheat, thus jeopardising the success of others. The sad and foolish thing is that many who make such great sacrifices to get to the top do so only to discover that it doesn't satisfy their deepest needs. Why, then, we might ask, do people so readily engage in unethical activities for such ephemeral gains? Surely, it is all meaningless. A chasing after the wind!

Power, popularity and success are often very short-lived, and we see this repeatedly in every area of society. Monarchs, political leaders or dictators are regularly replaced by others who in turn will go the way of their predecessors. It is like cutting off the head of a Hydra: another takes its place. No sooner do we remove one tyrant from the world than he or she is replaced by another. Business executives, entertainers and sport celebrities reach a peak in their career and then wane. The media time and again rapidly promote people to a high status, only to destroy them with bad publicity which may be true or false. Who knows when they might fall from their high position?

Remaining in a position of power and maintaining a high standard is extremely difficult. The Russian-born American composer Irving Berlin was right when he said, 'The toughest thing about success is that you've got to keep on being a success.'[1] That is far easier said than done. It can be incredibly tough at the top, and success today is no guarantee of success tomorrow. We must remember that the fickleness or instability of human nature means that people continually seek change. As a consequence, the time of a person's downfall may come at any time. Sooner or later, success will vanish and so it is ultimately meaningless.

Reaching a pinnacle of power can result in a lonely existence because it is very easy to become isolated from everyday life. It can become difficult to trust others, who often constantly indulge in flattery rather than reality. They say what their superior wants to hear, so as to gain approval and promotion, instead of what should be said. The lesson here for anyone in a position of power is obvious: Wise counsel is always better than undue praise. Frequent flattery can cause a person to bask in a world of adoration and adulation that will ultimately lead to disaster. Therefore, 'It is better to heed a wise man's rebuke than to listen to the song of fools.'[2] Wise counsel can make the difference between success and failure, war and peace, prosperity and poverty. And this fact should be a stern warning. Yet in spite of that there is a great danger that the honest critic will be rejected in favour of the one who flatters.

It is important for us to remember that communicative relationships, and not self-sufficiency, are essential for anyone to succeed. That is why in the book of Proverbs, Solomon writes, 'The way of a fool seems right to him, but a wise man listens to advice.'[3] Woodrow Wilson, the twenty-eighth President of the United States, once said, 'I not only use all the brains that I have, but all I can borrow.' Let us do the same because no one is wise enough to grasp the full meaning of every situation. Thus it follows that people who ignore good advice are not only a danger to themselves, but also to those beneath them. Such leaders have outlived their usefulness and will eventually be replaced by others or die a failure.

The ideal is to have leaders who are honest and efficient, but there are many instances of people in every generation who have abused their power. Indeed, wherever there is power there is the temptation to abuse it. In the Bible, we see that following the death of Solomon are a series of kings who were spiritually bad. Ahab, son of Omri, who succeeded his father, was worse than any of those before him.[4] He was a very weak man in a position of great power and that is always an extremely dangerous combination.

Since the time of Ahab, there have been many cold-blooded dictators who appear to be invincible while they rule, and then remarkably weak when they fall. It is a common fact of life that oppressive regimes rise and then fall. That is the cyclical, unchangeable nature of history. There is nothing new under the sun. It all has been done before.

Another fact that we must come to terms with is that the exploitation of the weak by oppressive regimes inevitably tends to filter through society. An ancient proverb says, 'A fish rots from the head down.' In like manner, corruption enters society through its heads of state and filters down through its citizens. Therefore soldiers, police, bureaucrats and anyone who can are likely to oppress and corrupt others in their struggle for survival. Their rationalising includes: 'Everybody is doing it, why shouldn't I?' There is, I believe, a common desire to dominate others in the gentlest human creature that lives. As Albert Camus remarked, 'We can't do without dominating others or being served .... Even the man on the bottom rung still has his wife, or his child. If he's a bachelor, his dog. The essential thing, in sum, is being able to get angry without the other person being able to answer back.'[5]

On the other hand, we should not automatically assume that it is always wrong to seek promotion and power. Quite the opposite! It can be good to have ambitions, providing that our motive is honourable. To aim for positions of responsibility and leadership so as to influence others and make things happen – or prevent things from happening – can be a great benefit to humanity. But how is this achieved? And why may I want a position of power? These are questions that need to be answered during our journey of discovery. If our honest answers are personal prestige and unlimited wealth, we shall ultimately fail to reach our destiny of lasting success. The simple truth is that those who are truly great do not allow sheer strength, coercion, selfishness or pride to be their guide. Instead, they rely on the ability to negotiate conflicts and to see things from other people's points of view. Disagreements need not necessarily turn into personal attacks.

It is certainly true that healthy ambition is based not primarily on self-gain but on self-sacrifice. A good and successful leader is always focused on the service he or she can render to other people. Paul in his letter to the Philippians has a fine comment on this: 'Do nothing out of selfish ambition or vain conceit. Rather, in humility value others above yourselves, not looking to your own interests but each of you to the interests of the others.'[6] That is the best answer to the question, 'How can I win true friends and influence people?' In sharp contrast, people who are self-centred and constantly craving honour and prestige for themselves will discover that their journey inevitably leads to loneliness and failure.

A pause for thought

A Danish proverb says, 'If envy were a fever, the entire world would be ill.' The English writer and clergyman Charles Caleb Colton said, 'For one man who sincerely pities our misfortunes, there are a thousand who sincerely hate our success.'[7] How do you respond to the success of others? Have you ever wished someone success but secretly wanted him or her to fail? To be truly successful in life, it must be realised that unhealthy comparisons and harmful competition with others needs to be avoided. You must love your neighbour as yourself.

9

PROVERBS AND WISDOM

Not only was the Teacher wise, but also he imparted knowledge to the people. He pondered and searched out and set in order many proverbs. The Teacher searched to find just the right words, and what he wrote was upright and true.

(Ecclesiastes 12:9,10).

Wisdom, like an inheritance, is a good thing
and benefits those who see the sun.
Wisdom is a shelter
as money is a shelter,
but the advantage of knowledge is this:
wisdom preserves those who have it.

(Ecclesiastes 7:11,12).

A PROVERB CAN VERY SIMPLY be defined as a short, pithy saying containing a general truth that can easily be understood and remembered. That being so, it can readily be passed on from one generation to another. During Elizabethan times their use was extremely popular, and schoolboys memorised hundreds of proverbs and maxims in English and in Latin. Partly it is a reflection of this cultural attitude that the plays of Shakespeare are so rich in proverbs. By the eighteenth century, however, the popularity of the proverb had declined. Yet, even in our sophisticated twenty-first century we still hear proverbs, many of ancient origin, being used in everyday conversation.

Who among us has not heard, 'Look before you leap'; 'Too many cooks spoil the broth'; 'A stitch in time saves nine'; 'Waste not, want not'; 'Chickens come home to roost'; 'Do not count your chickens before they are hatched'; or 'A bird in the hand is worth two in the bush'? These and numerous other proverbs contain wise advice which should be heeded and practised, for if we only quote them they are of no use. This is exactly what the poet John Keats is saying in a letter to George and Georgiana Keats (14 February–3 May 1819) when he wrote: 'Nothing ever becomes real till it is experienced – even a proverb is no proverb to you till your life has illustrated it.'

Some people would question the value of proverbs and claim that for almost every known proverb, you can find one that says the opposite. For example, if 'many hands make light work', can it also be correct to say that 'too many cooks spoil the broth'? Is it not logical to assume that two proverbs that seem to contradict one another cannot both possibly be true? Does not the contradiction question their value? Or to put it another way, does it convey a truth about the nature of reality?

The answer to this paradox is that life is contradictory, and therefore it follows that some proverbs will only be applicable to certain situations. Different action may be necessitated by changed circumstances and as a consequence: 'One man's meat will be another man's poison.' For example, in the book of Proverbs we read: 'Do not answer a fool according to his folly', but the next verse says, 'Answer a fool according to his folly'.[1] We are forbidden, and yet commanded to answer a fool. What, then, are we to do with this apparent contradiction of Scripture? The answer in this instance is easy to explain. Surely, in some situations it is appropriate that a fool's words should be answered so as to reveal the folly of what he or she has said. This, however, is not a rule for us in every situation. Sometimes it is better to be quiet. It clearly requires wisdom to know when we should speak, and when we should remain silent.

Proverbs provide us with wisdom for daily living and address the attitudes that face every generation. It should be no surprise, then, that proverbial expressions are commonly found in the Bible. The book of Proverbs, as the name suggests, is full of them. Many of these are quoted in the New Testament and many have found their way into everyday speech.

Some proverbial expressions simply consist of a short saying that has become familiar. A good example of this would be the words of King Ahab to King Ben-Hadad, 'One who puts on his armour should not boast like one who takes it off.'[2] Preparing for war is one thing and winning it another – it is the equivalent of saying, 'Do not count your chickens before they are hatched.'

The Hebrew word for 'proverb,' *mashal*, comes from a root meaning 'to be like'. This is appropriate, since many proverbs use comparison to teach their truths, as we see in Ecclesiastes 7. There the writer introduces a number of proverbs in which two groups of things are compared to show that one is much better than the other. For example, in verse 1: 'A good name is better than fine perfume, and the day of death better than the day of birth.' To what extent do you agree or disagree with these statements, and why?

Can anything in the first half of the above proverb prepare us for the shock of the second half? The reputation of a person is clearly more important than perfume, which can be used as a cover-up. Inward values are always more important than the outward appearance. But how can it be that the day of death is better than the day of birth? Such a thought to the vast majority of people appears to be illogical. Probably most of us are happy to think about our birthday and regard it as a time for celebration; but there is usually a great reluctance to talk about our death day. That is a serious mistake, for undoubtedly one of the greatest facts of life is death.

This theme of death continues in Ecclesiastes as we are told: 'It is better to go to a house of mourning than to go to a house of feasting, for death is the destiny of everyone; the living should take this to heart. Frustration is better than laughter, because a sad face is good for the heart. The heart of the wise is in the house of mourning, but the heart of fools is in the house of pleasure.' Evidently it will benefit people more to go to a funeral than to go to a party insofar that they are more likely to think about death and the purpose of life.

Ecclesiastes goes on to say, 'It is better to heed the rebuke of a wise person than to listen to the song of fools. Like the crackling of thorns under the pot, so is the laughter of fools. This too is meaningless.'

The thoughts of a wise person will be serious whilst the fool will think of nothing but trivia, merriment and laughter. Anything important will be an unmentionable subject in the company of fools. They can be likened to thorns that crackle and blaze, but within minutes the fire has gone. In the same way, the laughter of fools will produce no worthwhile result. The lesson is blazingly obvious. Avoid the company of fools.

Examination of the proverbs in Ecclesiastes 7 raises the question of whether or not they have anything in common. Yes, they certainly do! What, then, is their common feature? Surely it is this: they all reveal that a wise person is looking to the future and not just living in the present. For example, 'A good name is better than fine perfume'. Why is this? It is because the fragrance of the perfume lasts for only a very short time whilst a good name will persist. The wisdom to be found in the proverbs is applicable to us all. But how many people live only for the present and totally ignore their future? How unwise it is to have such a short-term outlook on life!

Wisdom is something very precious, and therefore something to be desired. 'Blessed are those who find wisdom, those who gain understanding, for she is more profitable than silver and yields better returns than gold. She is more precious than rubies; nothing you desire can compare with her.'[1] King Solomon, the author of Proverbs, clearly believed that it is far better to be wise than wealthy. Why is this so? It is simply because a wise person knows how to cope with the many difficulties of life. Wisdom can accomplish much more than can ever be achieved by brute strength,[4] weapons of war,[5] or material wealth. Even so, the vast majority of people today would probably disagree with this way of thinking. That is why it is often said, 'I want to be healthy, wealthy and wise.' More careful thought, however, will reveal that the priorities are in the wrong order. It would be better to say, 'I want to be wise, healthy and wealthy.'

Wisdom is something for which we should all strive. Indeed, it is no exaggeration to say that getting wisdom is the most important thing that we can do. So, how then is it obtained? The first essential step is to realise that true wisdom is much more than knowledge or intellectual ability; it is to have insight that is obtained only by revelation. Wisdom necessitates having insight so as to reach conclusions which are correct. This fact is well illustrated in the proverb, 'Foresight is better than hindsight, but insight is best.'

Although wisdom is much greater than knowledge it is important to learn all that we can so as to cope with life's frequent challenges. Nevertheless, history repeatedly reveals that education alone can be totally inadequate to deal with many problems. As Charles Caleb Colton rightly said, 'It is better to have wisdom without learning, than to have learning without wisdom; just as it is better to be rich without being the possessor of a mine, than to be the possessor of a mine without being rich.'[6] Stated this simply, we might be tempted to think that we are confronted with the problem of having to choose between possessing knowledge or wisdom. That, however, would be a serious mistake. It is possible for us to have both. But before going further, we need to pause because we are now about to enter into new and far more adventurous territory.

A pause for thought

Of all the qualities we need to achieve satisfaction, none is greater than wisdom. It allows us to build our lives on a firm foundation, inspires confidence, and enables us to handle difficult situations. Biblical proverbs provide timeless, concise, common sense advice for wise, successful daily living. 'The fear of the LORD is the beginning of wisdom, and knowledge of the Holy One is understanding.'[7] According to the Bible, it's not what we know, but who we know that's important.

10

GODLESS RELIGION

Guard your steps when you go to the house of God. Go near to listen rather than to offer the sacrifice of fools, who do not know that they do wrong.
Do not be quick with your mouth,
do not be hasty in your heart
to utter anything before God.
God is in heaven
and you are on earth,
so let your words be few.
A dream comes when there are many cares,
and many words mark the speech of a fool.
When you make a vow to God, do not delay to fulfil it. He has no pleasure in fools; fulfil your vow. It is better not to make a vow than to make one and not fulfil it. Do not let your mouth lead you into sin. And do not protest to the temple messenger, 'My vow was a mistake.' Why should God be angry at what you say and destroy the work of your hands? Much dreaming and many words are meaningless. Therefore fear God.

(Ecclesiastes 5:1–7)

URING OUR JOURNEY OF DISCOVERY, we have observed various important aspects of the meaninglessness of secular life 'under the sun'. Now, for the first time, we are to consider the subject of worship at the house of God; an 'above the sun' activity. The 'house of God' here referred to is undoubtedly the magnificent Temple at Jerusalem, though what follows would be equally applicable to any place where it is believed that God might reveal himself.

The author of Ecclesiastes turned his observant eye on those who went to the Temple to worship God. But what he saw deeply troubled him. These well-meaning people believed that God may be approached, addressed in prayer, and that he would accept their vows. It was very clear, however, from what was happening, that there are great dangers of making even these things a meaningless exercise. The attitude of these people in obeying the laws and the ordinances could appear to be outwardly irreproachable, even though inwardly their motive was clearly ritual rather than righteous. It is so easy for any one of us to go mechanically through the motions of religion, and apparently many people do, without ever experiencing the reality of it. In other words, the inward obedience does not run parallel to the outward observance; rather, it is outward obedience coupled with inward disobedience. Such a worldly approach to worship is foolish and absolutely worthless. But that is not all! These people possess a false sense of security because their actions are not based upon a solid foundation. Therefore the stern caution: 'Guard your steps when you go to the house of God.'

We see that there are many instances within the Old Testament where God was not worshipped as he should have been. For example: "'Even now," declares the LORD, "return to me with all your heart, with fasting and weeping and mourning." Rend your heart and not your garments. Return to the LORD your God, for he is gracious and compassionate, slow to anger and abounding in love, and he relents from sending calamity.'[1] The declaration to rend their hearts and not their garments reveals that there was a contradiction between what they professed to believe and the way they lived their lives. These people professed the love of God, but in practice their religion had become nothing more than a mere outward show of ceremonial self-righteousness. It was utterly meaningless.

A similar pattern emerges in the New Testament. There we see that reference is frequently made to the unacceptable worship which was offered by the Pharisees. This influential Jewish sect believed that God's standards were not those of ordinary society. For that reason they disciplined and deprived themselves so as to be prepared for their Day of Judgement. Unquestionably the Pharisees were people who meant serious business with God. They could truthfully say, 'God, I thank you that I am not like other people – robbers, evildoers, adulterers – or even like this tax collector. I fast twice a week and give a tenth of all I get.'[2]

The Pharisees sincerely believed that what they did was the right way to live before God. It was therefore understandable that they felt they were better than others. As a result they boasted about their superior goodness. But the fact of the matter is that they deceived themselves because they had a false concept of righteousness. They failed to realise that what really counts, as far as God is concerned, is what is found within a person. That is why Jesus said, 'Woe to you, teachers of the law and Pharisees, you hypocrites! You are like whitewashed tombs, which look beautiful on the outside but on the inside are full of the bones of the dead and everything unclean. In the same way, on the outside you appear to people as righteous but on the inside you are full of hypocrisy and wickedness.'[3]

What then, we might ask, should we expect to see in the worship of those who claim to be God's people today? Should their worship be formal or informal? My answer to this question is that formal worship can very easily become a ritualistic formality. On the other hand, informal worship may be nothing more than spiritual entertainment. Both forms taken to extreme are unacceptable because their priorities are wrong. Now, of course, either formal or informal worship would appear to be acceptable, providing that it glorifies God. But if not, it is all so meaningless, like chasing the wind. A very simple definition of godless religion is 'that which doesn't meet God when it comes to worship'. Sadly, from what we see, there is a vast amount of sterile and sentimental worship about.

In his book *The Living Church*, John Stott put it in these words:

> The church is not always conspicuous for the profound reality of its worship … We seem to have little sense of the greatness and glory of Almighty God. We do not bow down before him in awe and wonder. Our tendency is to be cocky, flippant and proud. We take little trouble to prepare our worship services. In consequence, they are sometimes slovenly, mechanical, perfunctory and dull. At other times they are frivolous, to the point of irreverence. No wonder those seeking reality often pass us by![4]

The noun 'worship' is a contraction of 'worth-ship'. Used as a verb, it means to 'acknowledge worth'. Thus to truly worship God is to wholeheartedly acknowledge his worth and worthiness. It would appear that this may be done successfully in many different ways, providing that it is sincere and biblical. In the early Church we see that its worship was joyful.[5] And there can be no doubt that this was one of the most potent factors in the rapid spread of Christianity. At the same time its worship, though often informal and spontaneous, was not irreverent. Quite the contrary! Everyone was filled with awe because they recognised the absolute authority and holiness of God.

Acceptable worship is never achieved by a multitude of words or by the observance of external rites and duties. It is evident throughout the Bible that worship should always be the humble acknowledgement of God's sovereignty in sincerity and truth. Jesus said, 'And when you pray, do not keep on babbling like pagans, for they think they will be heard because of their many words.'[6] That is not to say that a lengthy prayer is always wrong. The important point – and this should apply to everything in life – is the motive. Is it sincere? The simple fact is that what we say may not silence criticism, whereas good conduct will.

Some people think that the longer and the louder they pray, the more likely will be their chance of success in receiving what they want. A good example of this would be the priests of Baal. 'They called on the name of Baal from morning till noon. "Baal, answer us!" they shouted. But there was no response; no one answered …. So they shouted louder …. But there was no response, no one answered, no one paid attention.'[7] They even resorted to dancing wildly around the altar they had made and cut themselves with swords and spears, but all to no avail.

The author of Ecclesiastes also draws our attention to the serious problem of rash promises. Clearly there were people going to the Temple and foolishly saying things to their God that they did not mean. It is very easy to make a promise and then fail to keep it. Has any one of us ever done that? This raises the question: 'Why ever make a promise unless it is absolutely necessary?' The Bible says, 'If you make a vow to the LORD your God, do not be slow to pay it, for the LORD your God will certainly demand it of you and you will be guilty of sin. But if you refrain from making a vow, you will not be guilty. Whatever your lips utter you must be sure to do, because you made your vow freely to the LORD your God with your own mouth.'[8] God does not demand that we make vows to him, but if we do make them, then we have an obligation to honour our vows without unreasonable delay. Otherwise what began with good intentions can end in a serious offence.

There are some people who will deny the existence of a God. They believe that this universe evolved by chance, in other words by luck. That is the way it is and so worship will be irrelevant and meaningless to them, like chasing the wind. There is another group who do not know whether there is a God or not. Such people can never worship in sincerity and truth because they can't make up their minds. They waver back and forth in all they do. Some people worship a god other than God as described in the Bible. But ultimately this is useless, like chasing the wind. Then there are those who believe in a God who created and controls this universe, and it is their worship that is questioned.

Whatever we believe, at this stage of our journey, there can surely be no doubt that the use of the tongue plays a very important part in everyday life. All of us will sometimes say things which we later regret and cannot retract. Our tongue can be responsible for anger, criticism, exaggeration, gossip, slander, sarcasm and much more besides.

What we say is a result of what we think and it will inevitably, for better or worse, influence the course of our life. We should never underestimate the power of our speech, and remember that wise people refrain from speaking too freely. This great truth is well expressed in an ancient saying that goes something like this: 'Men have two ears but one tongue, that they should hear more than they speak. The ears are open, always ready to receive instruction; but the tongue is surrounded by a double row of teeth, to hedge it in, and to keep it within proper bounds.' Our basic education has taught us how to read, write and speak. Are we, however, educated in the art of listening?

A pause for thought

Why do people go to church? Is it because they are lonely and enjoy the company? Maybe they enjoy the music and the singing; while others may like to be intellectually stimulated by what is said. Do many people deceive themselves by adopting a routine that is lacking in spiritual reality?

11

BROADER HORIZONS

I have seen all the things that are done under the sun; all of them are meaningless, a chasing after the wind.

(Ecclesiastes 1:14)

A student wrote an alarming letter to his parents:

> Dear Mum and Dad,
>
> I have a lot to tell you. Because of the fire in my room started by rioting students, I suffered from smoke inhalation and had to be taken to hospital. While there I fell in love with a Chinese nurse. Then I was arrested for my part in the riots. Anyway, to cut a long story short, I am leaving university, getting married and moving to China.
>
> Your loving son,
>
> John
>
> PS None of the above happened, but I did fail my geography exam, and I wanted you to keep it in perspective.

We might query this student's way of revealing bad news to his parents. Nevertheless, it does teach us a very important lesson. That is, proper perspective is essential if we are going to reach satisfactory conclusions. Sometimes it is helpful for us to realise that our present problems pale in comparison to what they might have been.

The Concise Oxford Dictionary defines 'perspective' as 'a mental view of the relative importance of things'. But that, I believe, is often easier said than done. Things are not always as they first appear to be, because we fail to see the bigger picture. Hence, it can be a serious mistake to ignore the larger context of things and judge from present appearances alone.

Is not the lesson to be learned all too apparent? It is that people may observe the same situation and then react to it in an entirely different way. It has often been said that one person's problem is another person's opportunity, and that is true. There is such a thing as making a mountain out of a molehill by unduly exaggerating the severity of a situation. That is a serious mistake! To focus on the unimportant, and so overlook the important, will result in trivialities appearing to be insurmountable. Thus, nothing is ever achieved because it is considered to be too difficult. On the other hand, a lack of vision is likely to lead a person to make some very bad decisions.

The author of Ecclesiastes was a great observer of life in this world. He frequently says, 'I saw … ' As a result of his observations he asks himself many important questions about what, if anything, makes life worth living. But although he is asking all the right questions, he frequently arrives at the wrong answers. The reason for this is because he decided to look for the meaning of life within two very distinct boundaries. His vision was restricted to this earth and this life. So it should not be surprising that this near-sightedness would inevitably affect the outcome of his experiment to ascertain what life is all about. A much bigger view of the situation was essential to answer his unresolved questions.

First of all, in his search he put a limit on space. He looked for answers to his questions 'under the heavens' or 'under the sun'. This is a theme repeated many times by an author who does not waste words. On twenty-nine occasions he says, 'I've tried everything under the sun',[1] a phrase that occurs nowhere else in the Bible. Sometimes we hear people use that phrase today, suggesting that they have tried everything possible without success and do not know where to turn next.

The second limitation that he imposed on his search was that of time. He says, 'I wanted to see what was good for people to do under the heavens during the few days of their lives.'[2] There is no concept of life after death and so the overall picture is far from complete. Time has a way of changing our opinions because it allows us to see things from a different perspective. It would appear that if we are ever to satisfactorily answer the question, 'Is life worth living?' we must see beyond the observable world. Otherwise our preoccupation with the temporal rather than the eternal will inevitably lead to the unsatisfactory conclusion that everything in life is meaningless, a chasing after the wind.

It is unnecessary for us to ask, 'Is there death after life?' because death is one of the most obvious, inescapable realities of life. Our days on earth are certainly numbered. Therefore people who never trouble themselves asking 'Why?' are simply not facing reality. This raises the urgent question: when did you last have a serious talk in your family about death?

The American statesman Benjamin Franklin wrote, 'In this world nothing can be said to be certain, except death and taxes.'[3] Of course, he was wrong about taxes. Taxes can often be legally avoided or illegally evaded. But he was right about the certainty of death. Even the great advances in medical science and technology can at best only postpone the inevitable; we are all destined to die. As the theologian Fred Carl Kuehner so aptly comments, 'Death is the most democratic institution on earth ... It allows no discrimination, tolerates no exceptions. The mortality rate of mankind is the same the world over: one death per person.'[4] The author of Ecclesiastes says, 'There is a time for everything, and a season for every activity under the heavens: a time to be born and a time to die'.[5] The English philosopher, statesman and essayist Francis Bacon wrote, 'It is as natural to die as to be born.'[6] Accordingly, what we describe as living could just as appropriately be called dying.

If we confine our search to this earth and this life we will, according to those who believe in an afterlife, never satisfactorily understand the true purpose of our existence. A life lived 'under the sun', that is, only from a human point of view, will appear to be utterly meaningless. Thus it is understandable why many people are pessimistic about their future. Thankfully, I believe, this is not the whole story. If we can see 'above the sun', that is, to bring God into the equation, everything surely changes and the meaningless becomes meaningful. As G. Campbell Morgan comments, 'It is only as a man takes account of that which is over the sun as well as that which is under the sun that things under the sun are seen in their true light.'[7]

Does looking above the sun and beyond the grave really reveal the purpose of life? There are several ways to answer that question. Undoubtedly there are those who will say that human beings are annihilated at death and that the idea of an afterlife is just wishful thinking. The Roman writer Seneca said, 'There is nothing after death, and death itself is nothing.'[8] That is the way it is. Or is it? Must we accept death, live with it, and make the most of it before passing out of existence into nothingness?

Another group would say that they do not know whether there is an afterlife or not. Others are not asking that question. They avoid any talk about death as the Victorians avoided talk about sex. Many people today are reluctant to seriously think about death or the possibility of an afterlife. Why is this? I would suggest that there are several possible reasons. For example, it may be the fear of prolonged pain and suffering that are often associated with death. For others, there may be a fear of the unknown. There is no doubt in my mind that we feel much more comfortable in situations with which we are familiar, and death does not fit into such a category. To talk about death takes our journey into unknown and maybe dangerous territory.

It is probably true to say that most people accept the comforting and reassuring thought that there is some form of life after death. The British evangelist John Blanchard drew attention to this when he wrote:

> The ancient Egyptian *Book of the Dead* is among the oldest pieces of literature in the world – and life beyond the grave is one of its main themes. The coffins of those buried in the great pyramids were called 'the chests of the dead' and contained a map to guide the deceased on his journey. In ancient Greek religion a silver coin was placed in the dead person's mouth to pay the fare across the River Styx to Hades. Many other cultures have shown their belief in an afterlife by burying certain items with their corpses … Buddhism and Hinduism are two of the oldest surviving religions in the world, and both have a firm belief in the afterlife.[9]

The Bible is uncompromisingly clear that life continues beyond the grave. But how can we know that what it says is true?

A pause for thought

Is the thought of an afterlife a fantasy or a fact? Furthermore, is it possible to know one way or the other? Should we accept the philosophy of 'Eat, drink and be merry, for tomorrow we die' (see 1 Corinthians 15:32)? Or, is there perhaps more to the picture of life than we are seeing at present? On the next stage of our journey we will view some of the answers that have been given and try to determine whether life is meaningless or meaningful.

12

WHERE THERE'S LIFE, THERE'S HOPE

Anyone who is among the living has hope – even a live dog is
better off than a dead lion!
For the living know that they will die,
but the dead know nothing;
they have no further reward,
and even their name is forgotten.
Their love, their hate
and their jealousy have long since vanished;
never again will they have a part
in anything that happens under the sun.

(Ecclesiastes 9:4–6)

May the God of hope fill you with all joy and peace as you trust
in him, so that you may overflow with hope by the power of the
Holy Spirit.

(Romans 15:13)

P EOPLE HAVE OFTEN USED the word 'hope' to speak
of the expectation or desire for a certain thing to
occur. Today, however, we appear to put much
less emphasis on the 'expectation' component. We still
anticipate a desired end, but we are far from certain about
whether or not it will happen. For instance, 'I hope we

have good weather tomorrow, but I'm taking my coat and umbrella just in case it's bad.' Or, 'I hope to win the lottery, even though it's very unlikely.' Our hope, at times, may be nothing more than wishful thinking. It is to cling to a mere possibility that something nice may happen to us, but we are not sure of the result. Biblical hope is not like that. In the Bible, hope is a confident expectation of what God will do in the future based on his past promises and the amazing things he has already done. This is a hope that is certain.

While there is life, there is hope. Only the dead have none. Thus it is better to be a living dog than a dead lion. In this instance the lion, the king of beasts, has no hope, for he is dead. The dog, portrayed in the Bible as a despised scavenger and notorious for its uncleanness, has hope for he is still alive. Life affords a person a great opportunity to carefully consider the fact of death and to prepare for the future. Therefore, let us take advantage of this with a sense of urgency.

There is no escaping death when our time has come. One of the psalmists asks the question: 'Who can live and not see death, or who can escape the power of the grave?'[1] Death is the great leveller and, as we have seen so often during our journey, no serious-minded person can ignore that this demands a response. What then, should we do, or not do, in the meantime? Many people foolishly console themselves by deliberately avoiding the word 'death' as much as possible. Death is substituted with euphemistic phrases such as 'left us', or 'passed on', or 'fallen asleep'. It is said that Louis XV forbade his servants to use the word 'death' in his presence. But that was a silly mistake because no one can ever defeat death by trying to ignore or deny its existence.

What is the best response when things appear to be hopeless? Surely, the answer is to focus our thoughts on things that will last for ever. Hope causes us to adopt and develop a long-term perspective. We do not hope for something we already have. For if we already have something, we don't need to hope for it. Instead, we look to the future and to things which, being future, are as yet unseen. The apostle Paul reminds us that he considered his present problems to be relatively small when compared to the boundless weight of glory that awaited him. He had his sights firmly fixed not on what is seen, but on what was unseen, since what is seen is temporary, but what is unseen is permanent.[2]

According to the Bible, a Christian has a living Saviour who has conquered death. For example, the apostle Peter vividly describes our living hope in these words: 'Praise be to the God and Father of our Lord Jesus Christ! In his great mercy he has given us new birth into a living hope through the resurrection of Jesus Christ from the dead, and into an inheritance that can never perish, spoil or fade. This inheritance is kept in heaven for you, who through faith are shielded by God's power until the coming of the salvation that is ready to be revealed in the last time.'[3]

A hope that can be destroyed by death is hopeless. Hence, without the resurrection of Christ, any hope in him would be meaningless. But by rising from the dead, Jesus Christ has provided the assurance that we, too, can rise with him. Where there is life, there is hope. The next vital question to ask, however, is this: 'How can we corroborate these amazing claims?' Did Jesus Christ die to save sinners or did he not?

The death of Jesus about AD30 has undoubtedly become the most famous death in history. Why should that be? Certainly it has nothing to do with the method of execution. Crucifixion happened to a great many people in those days. The Roman general Varus crucified 2,000 following the death of Herod the Great in 4BC, and during the siege of Jerusalem the general Titus crucified so many fugitives from the city that neither 'room ... For the crosses, nor crosses for the bodies' could be found.[4] Jesus was crucified between two criminals. Why, then, is the cross of Jesus so unique? Why was his death so special?

The Bible tells us that Jesus had no sin,[5] and because it is sin that causes death,[6] there was no reason for him to die. Even so, he died! What is the answer to this great enigma? It is that he deliberately chose to die in a way that was not suicide: 'No one takes [my life] from me, but I lay it down of my own accord. I have authority to lay it down and authority to take it up again. This command I received from my Father.'[7] Thus, the voluntary aspect of the deed is clear. He could have escaped the cross at any time he wished,[8] but clearly chose not to do so. The reason for this should be obvious. Jesus knew that without the crucifixion there could be no resurrection and no reconciliation between God and a sinful world. This thought is well expressed by Paul in his letter to the Colossian Christians: 'Once you were alienated from God and were enemies in your minds because of your evil behaviour. But now he has reconciled you by Christ's physical body through death to present you holy in his sight, without blemish and free from accusation – if you continue in your faith, established and firm, and do not move from the hope held out in the gospel.'[9]

107

Jesus of Nazareth is a pivotal figure in history because he not only died a cruel death but, according to the Bible, was brought back to life by the power of God. Such a strong claim has never been made for any other person on this earth. But did Jesus actually die? That is a vital question we need to answer. And then if Jesus did die, was the resurrection true or false? We need to carefully examine the evidence upon which to base our verdict. There are some people who consider the resurrection to be fiction rather than fact. They regard themselves as far too sophisticated to accept such a possibility and therefore seek a natural explanation. One possibility is to believe in the so-called 'swoon' theory, whereby Jesus only fainted and was then revived in the cool of the tomb. Does not the fact that Jesus died in such a short time, about six hours, support this possibility? No, it certainly does not. The evidence supporting the death and resurrection of Jesus cannot satisfactorily be explained away by any logical process. It is a historical fact that Jesus was put to death in front of a large crowd. His executioners, who were soldiers, knew a dead man when they saw one. And to be absolutely certain, one of the soldiers pierced Jesus' side with a spear, and blood and water flowed out.[10] This is very strong medical proof of death. Not only that! We must consider that while he was being removed from the cross, prepared for burial and placed in the tomb, neither Joseph nor Nicodemus observed any sign of life. Are we to seriously believe that at some point during the next thirty-six hours Jesus recovered from a coma, pushed aside a very large stone, and evaded the armed guard?

It has also been suggested that the body was stolen from the tomb by a person or persons unknown. Tomb robbers were common at that time, but why would they not have taken the only things of any value – the grave clothes and spices? Why steal a naked body? Is it possible that the followers of Jesus removed his body and then proclaimed the story of the resurrection? Maybe the Roman or Jewish authorities, or someone else, moved the body without the Christians knowing about it. This was the immediate reaction of Mary Magdalene when she discovered that the tomb was empty.[11] It is difficult, however, to see what motive anyone would have to move the body.

Any natural explanation which attempts to deny the death and resurrection of Christ is not corroborated by the sheer force of evidence. Can you think of any good reason to ignore the testimony of the biblical authors and many eyewitnesses who said that he rose again from the dead? Independent witnesses provide clear evidence of several different resurrection appearances. Paul writes about some of these appearances: '... he appeared to Cephas [Peter], and then to the Twelve. After that, he appeared to more than five hundred of the brothers and sisters at the same time ... Then he appeared to James, then to all the apostles, and last of all he appeared to me also ...'[12] Sceptics might suggest that these sightings of Jesus were hallucinations, but the evidence is against this. A ghost has neither flesh nor bones.[13]

In reaching our final verdict we must also consider the fact that following the death of Jesus, and prior to the resurrection, the disciples were afraid and without hope. Peter was so terrified that he denied ever knowing Jesus.[14] But after the resurrection he and the other disciples spoke without fear of persecution or execution. Saul of Tarsus, who later became known as Paul, vehemently opposed Christianity until the risen Christ spoke to him. But what a change afterwards; he became a powerful evangelist.[15] Anyone who understands human nature knows that people do not react in such a way without some major influence. A thorough search for the truth reveals that the death and resurrection of Jesus is a historical event. No other verdict can be warranted by the sheer force of evidence.

A pause for thought

During our journey of discovery, we need to maintain a balanced view. For that reason, prejudice must always be avoided. Neither should we accept what others say without examination. We want to know the truth, the whole truth and nothing but the truth. Did Jesus Christ die to save sinners, or is it a lie? Was he buried, and was he raised from the dead on the third day, as the Scriptures say? How does this set Christianity apart from all other religions? What implications does this have for people today?

SOWING AND REAPING

Ship your grain across the sea;
after many days you may receive a return.
Invest in seven ventures, yes, in eight;
you do not know what disaster may come upon the land.
If clouds are full of water,
they pour rain upon the earth.
Whether a tree falls to the south or to the north,
in the place where it falls, there it will lie.
Whoever watches the wind will not plant;
whoever looks at the clouds will not reap.
As you do not know the path of the wind,
or how the body is formed in a mother's womb,
so you cannot understand the work of God,
the Maker of all things.
Sow your seed in the morning,
and at evening let your hands not be idle,
for you do not know which will succeed,
whether this or that,
or whether both will do equally well.

(Ecclesiastes 11:1–6)

A QUESTION OF INTERPRETATION IMMEDIATELY confronts us here. 'Ship your grain across the sea' is often interpreted as, 'Cast your bread upon the waters' (e.g. NKJV, ESV). It depends upon which Bible translation we use. The allusion in both instances, however, is to a long-term venture of faith. Michael Eaton expresses this well when he says, '(*Cast*) demands total commitment ... And has a forward look to it and (*you will find*), a reward which requires patience (*after many days*).'[1]

The general result of rewards and returns is that if we sow sparingly we will reap sparingly; sow generously and we will reap generously. Paul applies this 'law of the harvest' to the giving and sharing of resources.[2] If a person makes it a habit to give only a little, he or she can expect little in the way of blessings. On the other hand, those who habitually give generously will be greatly blessed. Therefore, someone might ask, 'Does that mean that we only give to get something in return?' The answer is, 'No, that would violate giving as an act of love!' But it would be wrong, I believe, to think that it is unworthy of a person to be interested in rewards. Even though the anticipation of a reward or the thought of a loss may not be the primary concern for doing or not doing something, it is a major characteristic of life. There is no shadow of doubt in my mind that all of us like to see a positive return from our investments.

It is true that if we want a harvest, we must sow our seed; otherwise there will be no harvest. Not only that, the kind of harvest we will get is predetermined by the type of seed we sow. If we sow lettuce seed we will get a lettuce crop; if we sow tomato seed we will get a tomato crop. It does not stop there! Good seed will produce a good crop, and bad seed will produce a bad crop. Exactly the same principle operates in the moral and spiritual sphere. 'Whoever sows to please their flesh, from the flesh will reap destruction; whoever sows to please the Spirit, from the Spirit will reap eternal life. Let us not become weary in doing good, for at the proper time we will reap a harvest if we do not give up.'[3]

A fact that we must come to terms with is that people eventually reap what they sow. Thus, it follows that anybody who is preoccupied with material things and so fails to develop an attitude of generosity will inevitably fail to achieve his or her full potential. In contrast, those who are generous are blessed, but it would be wrong to think of these blessings as always being material. What, then, can those who are generous expect? There are many benefits. For instance, it will help develop true friendships. And true friends will always come to our aid in times of need. If we have not helped others, the likelihood is that they will not help us.

The author of Ecclesiastes suggests that we do not put all our resources into one venture and it is easy to understand why. It would be foolish to risk losing everything by placing all our effort into one uncertain course of action. '[For] you do not know' is a key phrase.[4] But even though we do not know the unpredictability of a venture, it must not instil us with fear to such a degree that we never do anything. Rather, it should remind us to be cautious in what we decide to do.

To invest in seven or eight ventures is not to be taken literally. Such language in the Bible often denotes an indefinite number and therefore indicates that we should do as much as we can. Investing in many ventures of faith means that at least some should give a good return on our investment. This is the equivalent of saying: 'Don't put all your eggs in one basket.' Or as Roger Norman Whybray says, '[He] is advising readers to take the risk involved in sea-trade (v.1), but also to spread the risk by sending the goods in separate consignments (v.2).'[5]

It is impossible for any of us to know 'what disaster may come upon the land' and so the opportunity for doing well is uncertain. We may at any time be deprived of our wealth and so no longer be in a position to give. Indeed, there are people who will use this argument as an excuse for not giving to the needy. They believe that difficult times may lie ahead and so they adopt a covetous attitude to protect themselves for the future. 'What is the point of giving to someone else?' they say. This was the attitude of the foolish and wicked Nabal who, having received a reasonable request, said, 'Why should I take my bread and water, and the meat I have slaughtered for my shearers, and give it to men coming from who knows where?'[26] Nabal's ungenerous attitude would certainly have led to disaster had it not been for the timely intervention of his wife.

A generous person is likened in Ecclesiastes to a cloud full of precious water which empties itself upon the earth to make it fruitful. Hence, considering the fact that the clouds are bountiful to the earth which is so far below them surely challenges us to give what we can to our neighbour who is so close.

Clouds full of water pouring rain are an expected event. In contrast, if a tree falls to the south or the north it is most likely unexpected. This reminds us that some things in life we can see coming whilst other things can, and do, take us completely by surprise. So, how do we react? The answer is that it depends on how we see things. It is a fact that people can see the same situations and interpret them in entirely different ways. We noticed earlier on our journey that one person's problem may be another person's opportunity. The natural eye may see nothing but a gathering storm and the possibility of disaster. But the eye of faith can see beyond this life. People who trust in God know that he is in complete control. Furthermore, they know that God will provide them with the necessary strength to continue when life seems too hard or obstacles seem too great.

Situations that confront us are often shrouded with uncertainty and so the outcome will not always be obvious. It is not possible for us to know the ultimate destination of the wind. It cannot even be seen. We hear its sound, but we cannot tell where it comes from or where it is going. Be that as it may, those who believe that God controls the wind are not deterred. But 'Whoever watches the wind will not plant', which signifies giving; 'whoever looks at the clouds will not reap', which signifies receiving. If we magnify every little difficulty so that we are afraid to plant until the wind blows exactly in the right direction, if we are afraid to reap because the clouds indicate unfavourable weather, we shall lose the opportunity and never accomplish anything worthwhile.

There are many things that we do not understand. For example, we do not know 'how the body is formed in a mother's womb'. Even though there are tremendous advances in research, there are still many things that cannot be fully explored or explained. Science can try to tell us how the world began, but it has no methods for answering the crucial questions, 'Who created the world, and why?' It is impossible for us to fully understand the work of God in his creation. It is impossible for a finite being to fully understand the workings of an infinite God. Certain things which happen to us often defy explanation. We may have been confident of success and failed miserably. Or the odds may have been overwhelmingly against us and we experienced great success. At the time we do not always understand the outcome of a situation and have to wrestle with the question, 'Why?'

What is the correct response to uncertainty? Surely, it is to realise that life is an adventure of faith and that it is necessary to use our time wisely. To put it very simply, we are to sow our seed in the morning and work hard at all times. Our commitment must be continuous, willing and wholehearted. The reason is because we do not know which of our tasks will succeed. If the seed sown in the morning produce nothing, there may be something to reap from that sown in the evening. It may be that they will do equally well.

Sowing seed and then reaping a harvest takes time. It can be a very slow process from sowing to fruition, and so it is necessary to be patient. It is also necessary to be confident that the seed will grow and reproduce itself. There is life in a seed that never ceases to amaze us. Tall oaks develop from little acorns. How a tiny seed does this is beyond our comprehension. All that we can do is to provide the ideal growing conditions and then wait patiently.

Like a seed, the Bible message has the power to produce new life in people. This fact alone should be sufficient to attract our serious attention. But why should anyone accept that what the Bible teaches is true? In answer to this question, John MacArthur says this:

> I believe the Bible is true because it gives me the experience that it claims it will give me. For example, the Bible says that God will forgive my sins. I believe that. I accepted God's forgiveness and it happened. How do I know? I have a sense of freedom from guilt ... Yes, the Bible really changes lives. Millions of people – from great heads of state to brilliant educators and scientists, from philosophers and writers to generals and historians – could all testify about how the Bible has changed their lives.[7]

Maybe it will be a considerable time before there are any noticeable signs of growth, but God can make it happen.

Paul is well aware of this and that is why he says to the Corinthians, 'I planted the seed, Apollos watered it, but God has been making it grow. So neither the one who plants nor the one who waters is anything, but only God, who makes things grow.'[8] Whatever the evidence, it is only by power imparted by the Holy Spirit that a person is able to turn to God in true faith. Nothing of what the Bible says is of any use if someone doesn't desire to be convinced. This is what Martyn Lloyd-Jones had in mind when he wrote, 'Ultimately this question of the authority of the Scriptures is a matter of faith and not argument ... you may convince a man intellectually of what you're saying, but still he may not of necessity believe in and accept the authority of the Scripture.'[9]

The Great Commission

Those who truly believe the good news that God saves people through the work of Jesus Christ have a duty to tell others who do not yet know him. Jesus said, '[G]o and make disciples of all nations, baptising them in the name of the Father and of the Son and of the Holy Spirit, and teaching them to obey everything I have commanded you. And surely I am with you always, to the very end of the age.'[10] These words are applicable to all Christians. Without the power of God, all our knowledge, work or anything else will be meaningless, like chasing the wind. But for those who are obedient to God's commands, there is the promise of his constant presence until that great day when they shall be glorified with him for ever. Meanwhile, there is an immense opportunity to serve God. 'The harvest is plentiful but the workers are few.'[11]

A pause for thought

Our short journey together has revealed that much of what we do in life is very closely interrelated. For example, those who are genuinely concerned about the needs of others will develop healthy relationships. In dramatic contrast, those who are always greedy for more will experience a breakdown of relationships that is inevitably followed by loneliness. It is impossible to sow one thing and reap the opposite, or even something else. People will eventually reap what they sow.

14

CONCLUDING THOUGHTS

Now all has been heard;
here is the conclusion of the matter:
fear God and keep his commandments,
for this is the duty of all mankind.
For God will bring every deed into judgment,
including every hidden thing,
whether it is good or evil.

(Ecclesiastes 12:13,14)

A S WE NEAR THE END OF our short journey of
discovery, it is necessary to again ask the
fundamental question: 'Is life worth living?' This
is the question the author of Ecclesiastes was determined to
answer by his pursuit of knowledge, professional success,
social position, pleasure, possessions and projects. And
following a very careful and unprejudiced investigation
of 'life under the sun', he decided, 'No, life is not worth
living.' He gave various reasons to support his answer. For
instance, he saw the futility of wisdom, of work, and of
wealth, because of physical death that inevitably comes to

everyone. Is this it, then? Case closed! No, being a wise person, he decided to look at the problem from another perspective. He brought God into the picture and saw that life did have a purpose. He came to realise that life was not monotonous, and that what had appeared to be meaningless now became meaningful.

Our attention is now focused heavenward with a sense of great urgency. He says, 'Remember your Creator in the days of your youth'.[1] How does that grab us? If we accept that God is our Creator, relinquish our pretence of self-sufficiency and fully commit ourselves to him, it will surely determine how we conduct our lives. Furthermore, there can be no time when this can be done to greater advantage than whilst we are young. Indeed, the brevity of life should be a strong incentive for us to make the most of every opportunity.

It is sometimes said that 'life begins at forty'. This was the title of a self-help book by the American psychologist Walter B. Pitkin. Later the phrase became the title of a popular song by Jack Yellen and Ted Shapiro, recorded by Sophie Tucker in 1937. We might ask, 'If life did begin at forty, what is it that ends at thirty-nine?' Of course, a life worth living does not necessarily begin at forty, fifty, sixty, seventy or any other age. For some people, life will always appear to be monotonous and utterly meaningless. Why is this? Is there no escape from a life that appears to be going absolutely nowhere? Yes, I am convinced that there is.

For life to be truly satisfying, it has to have a sense of purpose. If life has no purpose, it is not worth living. It is meaningless, like chasing the wind. For that reason the author of Ecclesiastes closes where he began. "'Meaningless! Meaningless!' says the Teacher. "Everything is meaningless!'"[2] Again, this raises the urgent question: 'How can I experience real, lasting happiness under the sun?'

The story is told of a mother saying to her son, 'Be good and be happy.' He replies, 'Please make up your mind!' That, of course, is a wrong assumption. Being good and being happy are not, as some people would have us believe, incompatible. Quite the opposite is true! 'This is what I have observed to be good: that it is appropriate for a person to eat, to drink and to find satisfaction in their toilsome labour under the sun during the few days of life God has given them – for this is their lot.'[3] The key word here is 'God', and the secret of life is to accept that he has given these things as gifts for us to enjoy. God is not a cosmic killjoy who impoverishes people's lives. If, however, we devote ourselves exclusively to the pursuit of pleasure or sensual gratification it will never produce true joy and lasting satisfaction. The reason for this is that it is impossible to satisfactorily benefit from the gifts of God aloof from the God who gives the gifts.

People have various views of God which are often contradictory to each other. That is why there are many different religions. So the vital question is: which, if any, is the true God? Think carefully about this because it has serious consequences. The Bible presents us with a God who created and controls our universe. But why should we believe that what the Bible says is true? A powerful answer to this question would be its numerous fulfilled prophecies. Read what the Bible predicts about Babylon, Tyre, Sidon, Sodom and Gomorrah and then see what happened. There are precise predictions about Jesus, from his birth to his ascension, that according to many eyewitnesses have all been proved to be true. What about the predictions such as a new heaven and a new earth that have not occurred? The simple answer is that there is still time for these things to happen.

The author of Ecclesiastes refers to God forty times and always uses the word 'Elohim' rather than 'Jehovah'. This is to be expected since he is dealing with what he sees 'under the sun'. He views life as a man who knows and worships God as the almighty, glorious God of creation who exercises his sovereign power. The name 'LORD' (Jehovah) is the equivalent of Redeemer-Saviour; a God who graciously reveals himself to sinful people. When we reach the final command of Ecclesiastes, 'fear God and keep his commandments' (12:13), we are ready to be introduced to Christ the Redeemer. "As the law was designed to lead men to Christ, so this book was written to lead those 'under the sun' to the Son (cf. Hebrews 1:1)."[4]

Faith in the incarnate Son of God

Eternal life is a gift which God gives to those who believe in his Son and, according to the Bible, it may be found nowhere else. 'Whoever has the Son has life; whoever does not have the Son of God does not have life.'[5] That is a clear statement about the spiritual state of all humanity on this earth. As we turn the pages of the New Testament we find that Jesus is the Messiah, the Son of God, and that by believing in him we will have life.[6] We will know why we are here on earth and we will know where we are going.

There will be those who claim that Jesus, although a pivotal figure in human history, was just a man. Such a verdict, however, is not supported by the Bible, which overwhelmingly states that Jesus is the Son God. He is not merely a son of God, but the Son of God, 'the one and only Son, who came from the Father, full of grace and truth.'[7] For over 2,000 years, his life and teaching have drawn countless millions from all walks of life into accepting him as the Saviour of the world.

Now, at this stage of our journey, some may ask how people who lived in Old Testament times could have been saved. The answer is straightforward. In Romans 4, Paul makes it abundantly clear that they were saved by grace through faith. They looked forward to the prophesied coming Messiah and those who exercised faith were saved. Today we can look back to the person and work of Christ on the cross with the assurance that anyone who believes in him is given the blessings of salvation. All that is required is faith in Christ.

The primary message of Ecclesiastes is, therefore, not a confession of failure or disappointment. Rather it is a work inspired by the Holy Spirit and consequently without error.[8] It directs us to God who alone can satisfactorily fulfil our every need. Therefore, not surprisingly, the final conclusion is that we should 'fear God and keep his commandments, for this is the duty of all mankind'. 'The fear of the LORD is the beginning of wisdom, and knowledge of the Holy One is understanding.'[9]

What is God really like? The Bible says that he is 'compassionate and gracious, slow to anger, abounding in love'.[10] Even so, these attributes should not be given emphasis in ways that make us forget that God is also a God of holiness and therefore a God of wrath. He will not tolerate sin. That is why God told the people of Israel, 'I will bless you if you obey me and I will curse you if you do not' and history reveals that they experienced both.[11] It is sometimes said that 'God hates sin but loves the sinner'. But such a statement is unbiblical. God hates sinners too, if they hold on to their sin and refuse to be separated from it.

The above picture of God is contrary to what many people imagine he is like. Surely, they argue, it would be impossible for a God of love to allow anyone to experience eternal conscious suffering in hell. That is not a loving thing to do; so God could never do it. If that is so then Heinrich Heine would have been justified when he said on his deathbed, 'God will pardon me. It is his trade.' After a lifetime of sin he obviously had no reverent fear of God.

A healthy fear of God will enable us to keep our perspective of where we need to be in our relationship with him. The message proclaimed by many preachers, 'God is love and God loves you' is a too simplistic, sentimental view of God and inevitably leads people to think like Heine.

This is a grave mistake. God's dominant characteristic is not his love but his holiness. The British evangelist John Blanchard has written, 'When we understand God's holy hatred of sin, perhaps the more relevant question is not "How can a God of love send anyone to hell?" but "How can a God of holiness allow anyone into heaven?"'[12] The prophet Habakkuk acknowledged this truth by crying out to God, 'Your eyes are too pure to look on evil; you cannot tolerate wrongdoing.'[13]

God makes laws for his kingdom. For example, when he brought his people out of Egypt he gave them laws – the Ten Commandments.[14] If people are to live together in harmony it is essential to have laws. Even those who are isolated from society still have to live in the presence of God and so there are commands about respecting his name and his day. 'You shall not misuse the name of the LORD your God, for the LORD will not hold anyone guiltless who misuses his name. Remember the Sabbath day by keeping it holy.'[15] For any law to be effective there must be a deterrent. At a social level people may receive a warning, a fine, imprisonment or execution. There is only one penalty attached to God's law and that is death. The Bible says that 'all have sinned and fall short of the glory of God'[16] and that 'the wages of sin is death, but the gift of God is eternal life in Christ Jesus our Lord'.[17]

Some may wonder at this point if God will punish or pardon sin. The answer is that he can do both, and if that appears to be a contradiction to anyone it is because they do not understand the meaning of the cross. It is at the cross that the law and the love, the justice and the mercy of God operate together, and where, as one of the psalms beautifully expresses it, 'Love and faithfulness meet together; righteousness and peace kiss each other.'[18] It is at the cross that Jesus fulfilled all the demands of God's law, so that we, who are sinful and destined for the everlastingness of hell, are acquitted and heading for eternal life in heaven. The eternal and unchanging love of God through Jesus Christ is the only way that leads to a life of holiness. But how do people respond to him who paid such an immeasurable price to save them from the punishment they deserve?

Paul speaking to the Athenians said, "'For he [God] has set a day when he will judge the world with justice by the man he has appointed. He has given proof of this to everyone by raising him [Jesus] from the dead.'' When they heard about the resurrection of the dead, some of them sneered, but others said, "We want to hear you again on this subject.'" Others 'believed'.[19] People react in exactly the same way today. There is nothing new under the sun. History merely repeats itself.

131

The author of Ecclesiastes believed that without God, a person's efforts are ultimately useless and life is meaningless. Likewise, if we are honest in interpreting our observations throughout this journey, we will also realise that life without God is ultimately useless – a chasing after the wind. We need to seriously ask ourselves, 'Can we truly acknowledge Jesus Christ as our Saviour and Lord?'

Believing in Jesus Christ is not only to accept that what the Bible says is true. To such an invitation there must be a positive response. Therefore, 'Lord, save me' must be our sincere prayer. 'And everyone who calls on the name of the Lord will be saved.'[20] Can any one of us afford to be undecided or indifferent to such a vital decision? The Bible makes it abundantly clear what our response should be:

Seek the LORD while he may be found; call on him while he is near.[21]

The all-important thing is not to let this opportunity pass by. The time to seek is now!

NOTES

CHAPTER 1: GOING NOWHERE

1. Elliot Jaques, 'Death and the Midlife Crisis', *International Journal of Psychoanalysis*, 1965.

CHAPTER 2: THE SEARCH FOR SATISFACTION

1. Edmund Burke, *Reflections on the Revolution in France*, New York: OUP, 1993.

2. George Wilhelm Hegel, *Lectures on the Philosophy of World History*, Cambridge: CUP, 1976.

3. Ecclesiastes 2:1–3.

4. Aldous Huxley, 'Do What You Will', *Holy Face*, 1929.

5. Paul Du Noyer interviews Van Morrison and Spike Milligan, *Q Magazine*, August 1989.

6. 'Books', *Newsweek*, 3 November 1975.

7. Job 1:21.

8. Ecclesiastes 2:18,19, NIV 1984.

CHAPTER 3: A TIME FOR EVERYTHING

1. Robert Burns, (1759–96), 'Tam O'Shanter'.
2. Robert Herrick, (1591–1674), 'To the Virgins, to Make Much of Time'.
3. William Ernest Henley, (1849–1903), 'Invictus'.
4. See Luke 12:16–21.
5. Proverbs 27:1.

CHAPTER 4: LIFE'S NOT FAIR

1. Matthew 20:1–16.
2. Habakkuk 1:2–4.
3. Joseph Joubert, *Pensées* (1842). Quoted by Benjamin Disraeli in a speech, 'Agricultural Distress', 11 February 1851.
4. Matthew 26:14,15.
5. Matthew 26:59.
6. Charles Caleb Colton, *Lacon* (1825), 2.6.
7. Numbers 11:15; 1 Kings 19:4; Jonah 4:3; 2 Corinthians 1:8.

CHAPTER 5: THE RAT RACE

1. Erich Fromm, *Escape from Freedom*, chapter 4, New York: Holt, Winehart and Winston, 1941.
2. Proverbs 6:10; 24:33.
3. Philippians 2:3,4.

CHAPTER 6: THE LOVE OF MONEY

1. Ecclesiastes 5:12, NIV 1984.
2. Roland Murphy, *Ecclesiastes*, Word Bible Commentary, Word Books, p. 52.
3. 1 Timothy 6:10.
4. Warren W. Wiersbe, *Be Satisfied*, Colorado Springs, CO: David C. Cook, 2010, p. 91.
5. Acts 20:35.

CHAPTER 7: ADVANTAGES OF COMPANIONSHIP

1. Genesis 2:18.
2. David Wigg, *Mail Online*, 12 October 2012.
3. Matthew 14:23; Mark 6:46; Luke 6:12.
4. 1 Samuel 16:14–23.
5. 1 Samuel 28:1–20.
6. 1 Kings 1:1–4.
7. Luke 16:1–9.

CHAPTER 8: A POSITION OF POWER

1. Irving Berlin, *Theatre Arts*, February 1958.
2. Ecclesiastes 7:5, NIV 1984.
3. Proverbs 12:15, NIV 1984.
4. 1 Kings 16:30.
5. Albert Camus, *The Fall*, New York: Borzoi Books, 1956.

6. Philippians 2:3,4.

7. Charles Caleb Colton, *Lacon* (1825), 1. 507.

CHAPTER 9: PROVERBS AND WISDOM

1. Proverbs 26:4,5.

2. 1 Kings 20:11.

3. Proverbs 3:13–15.

4. Ecclesiastes 9:16.

5. Ecclesiastes 9:18.

6. Charles Caleb Colton, *Lacon* (1825), 2.26.

7. Proverbs 9:10.

CHAPTER 10: GODLESS RELIGION

1. Joel 2:12,13.

2. Luke 18:11,12.

3. Matthew 23:27,28.

4. John Stott, *The Living Church*, Downers Grove, IL: Inter-Varsity Press, 2007, p. 45.

5. Galatians 5:22. People who are filled with the Spirit will be joyful because they look beyond the problems of daily life to their future glory. Joy is a fruit of the Spirit.

6. Matthew 6:7.

7. 1 Kings 18:25–29.

8. Deuteronomy 23:21–23.

CHAPTER 11: BROADER HORIZONS

1. Ecclesiastes 1:3,9,14; 2:11,17,18,19,20,22; 3:16; 4:1,3,7,15; 5:13,18; 6:1,12; 8:9,15 (twice),17; 9:3,6,9 (twice),11,13; 10:5.

2. Ecclesiastes 2:3b.

3. Letter to Jean Baptiste Le Roy, 13 November 1789. *Writings*, vol. x.

4. Fred Carl Kuehner, 'Heaven and Hell', in *Fundamentals of the Faith*, ed. Carl F.H. Henry, *Christianity Today*, p. 24c.

5. Ecclesiastes 3:1,2a.

6. Francis Bacon, 'Of Death', *Essays*, 1625.

7. G. Campbell Morgan, *Unfolding Message of the Bible*, Grand Rapids, MI: Fleming H. Revell Company, 1961, p. 229.

8. Seneca, *Trojan Women*, trans. Frank Justus Miller, New York: Cornell University Press, 1986.

9. John Blanchard, *Whatever Happened to Hell?* Darlington: Evangelical Press, 1993, p. 63.

CHAPTER 12: WHERE THERE'S LIFE, THERE'S HOPE

1. Psalm 89:48.

2. 2 Corinthians 4:17,18.

3. 1 Peter 1:3–5.

4. Accounts given by Josephus in *Antiquities* xvii. 10.10 and *Jewish War* V xi 1.

5. 2 Corinthians 5:21; 1 Peter 2:22.

6. Romans 6:23.

7. John 10:18.

8. Matthew 26:49–54.

9. Colossians 1:21–23a.

10. John 19:34.

11. John 20:2.

12. 1Corinthians 15:5–8.

13. Luke 24:35–43.

14. Matthew 26:69–75.

15. Acts 9:1–22.

CHAPTER 13: SOWING AND REAPING

1. Michael Eaton, *Ecclesiastes*, Downers Grove, Illinois: Inter-Varsity Press, 1983, p. 140.

2. 2 Corinthians 9:6.

3. Galatians 6:8,9.

4. Ecclesiastes 11:2,5,6.

5. R.N. Whybray, *Ecclesiastes*, The New Century Bible Commentary, Grand Rapids, MI: William B. Eerdmans, p. 159.

6. 1 Samuel 25:11.

7. John MacArthur, *Why Believe the Bible?*, Ventura, CA: Regal Books, second edition, 2007, p. 25.

8. 1 Corinthians 3:6,7.

9. D. Martyn Lloyd-Jones, 'Authority of the Scriptures', *Decision*, June 1963.

10. Matthew 28:19,20.

11. Matthew 9:37.

CHAPTER 14: CONCLUDING THOUGHTS

1. Ecclesiastes 12:1a.

2. Ecclesiastes 12:8.

3. Ecclesiastes 5:18.

4. Wick Broomall, 'Ecclesiastes', Grand Rapids, MI: *Zondervan's Pictorial Bible Dictionary*, 1999.

5. 1 John 5:12.

6. John 20:31.

7. John 1:14.

8. 2 Timothy 3:16.

9. Proverbs 9:10.

10. Psalm 103:8.

11. Deuteronomy 28.

12. John Blanchard, *Whatever Happened To Hell?* Darlington: Evangelical Press, 1993, p. 170.

13. Habakkuk 1:13a.

14. Exodus 20:1–17.

15. Exodus 20:7,8.

16. Romans 3:23.

17. Romans 6:23.

18. Psalm 85:10
19. Acts 17:31–34.
20. Acts 2:21
21. Isaiah 55:6.